W9-BZM-350

DATE DUE			

Richard Hooker

Twayne's English Authors Series

Arthur F. Kinney, Editor
University of Massachusetts, Amherst

TEAS 350

RICHARD HOOKER
(1554–1600)
Engraving by William Faithorne
Courtesy of the Humanities Research Center,
The University of Texas at Austin

Richard Hooker

By Stanley Archer

Texas A & M University

Twayne Publishers • *Boston*

Richard Hooker

Stanley Archer

Copyright © 1983 by G. K. Hall & Company
All Rights Reserved
Published by Twayne Publishers
A Division of G. K. Hall & Company
70 Lincoln Street
Boston, Massachusetts 02111

Book Production by Marne B. Sultz

Book Design by Barbara Anderson

Printed on permanent/durable acid-free
paper and bound in the United States of
America.

Library of Congress Cataloging in
Publication Data

Archer, Stanley.
    Richard Hooker.

      (Twayne's English authors series; TEAS 350)
      Bibliography: p. 131
      Includes index.
      1. Hooker, Richard, 1553 or 4-1600. I. Title.
II. Series.
BX5199.H813A73   1983   230'.3'0924 [B] 83–230
ISBN 0–8057–6836–X

To
M. L. A.

Contents

About the Author

Stanley Archer is a professor of English at Texas A&M University, where he has been a faculty member since 1962. He received his B.A. from Texas A&M in 1959 and in the fall of that year went to the University of Mississippi as a Woodrow Wilson Fellow (Honorary) and N.D.E.A. Fellow. He received an M.A. in 1961 and a Ph.D. in 1965. His publications, primarily on seventeenth-century English literature, have appeared in *ELH*, *English Language Notes*, *The Explicator*, *Milton Quarterly*, *Notes and Queries*, *Papers on Language and Literature*, *Restoration and Eighteenth Century Theatre Research*, and *SCMLA Studies*.

Editor's Note

Stanley Archer's introductory study of the life and works of Richard Hooker shows the projected organization of all eight books of the *Lawes of Ecclesiastical Politie*, a cornerstone of the Elizabethan Settlement, summarizes their contents, and suggests in what ways Hooker's thought was influenced not only by Aristotle and the medieval scholastics but also by his own patrons John Jewel and John Whitgift. Separate chapters examine Hooker's minor works and his rich legacy for the later English Renaissance, particularly in matters of periodic rhetoric.

Arthur F. Kinney

Preface

Richard Hooker belongs in that category of authors who are more honored than read, whose work deserves rather than demands the reader's attention. For a modern reader, the first encounter with Hooker occurs in all likelihood through an anthology, for his work readily lends itself to publication by excerpts. The book upon which his reputation depends, the treatise *Of the Laws of Ecclesiastical Polity*, grew out of religious controversy during the Renaissance, a conflict distant in time and remote from modern modes of thought. To defend the established Church of England he produced a treatise of half a million words. At the risk of oversimplification, one might characterize it as prose of knowledge rather than power, of intellect rather than emotion. He writes of what he thinks and believes, not what he feels and imagines.

A major purpose of this study is to clarify Hooker's themes and ideas, their organization, and their theoretical foundations. The first chapter provides a biographical account with some attention to the cultural, historical, and intellectual currents that developed his character and influenced his career. Although there exists a considerable mass of biographical detail related to Hooker, one does not find, either in his writings or in accounts of his life by others, the kind of evidence that provides significant psychological insight. The available evidence does appear to indicate that Izaak Walton, who erred so often with detail, achieved in the seventeenth century a credible likeness of Hooker's character.

The second chapter is devoted to the minor works—sermons, a pamphlet, and fragments—since some of them were composed before the treatise. These works are more concerned with theology than the treatise, they clarify his thought on significant theological questions, and they throw some light upon subjects treated in the major work. I have grouped the sermons thematically and have attempted to explain important parallels to *Ecclesiastical Polity*, as well as differences.

Since *Ecclesiastical Polity* divides readily into three parts, I have devoted the next three chapters to the treatise. Books 1–4, the most familiar portion, are dealt with in the third chapter, where I attempt to clarify Hooker's major assumptions and values and to characterize his intellectual perspective. In chapter 4, devoted to the unwieldy fifth book, I have sought to make apparent the organization, to identify the axioms established at the outset, and to show how Hooker applies them. In the fifth chapter, which concerns the final three books on power, I examine the question of their authenticity and clarify Hooker's arguments in favor of the status quo in both religion and politics. The final chapter attempts to place Hooker in English literary history and offers a tentative assessment.

A further purpose of this book is to provide a perspective on important critical questions related to Hooker's work. These vary from specific matters such as the status of texts to larger questions of coherence and consistency. In examining these, I have made assumptions that seem central to an understanding of Hooker's work, assumptions whose influence will be readily apparent throughout. Scholars of Hooker may disagree with them, but will not find them new or surprising. First, I assume that his fundamental philosophical orientation is Aristotelian, with some overlay of Scholasticism. Whether the influence comes directly or indirectly, so frequent are the references and parallels to Aristotle that to ignore them is to miss a profound philosophical influence upon his work. My second assumption is that traditional English apologetics influenced Hooker more strongly than is usually realized. He stands in a line of apologists for the Church of England that originates with John Jewel and continues through John Whitgift. His debt to contemporary apologists, of whom there were many, does not equal that to his two most important predecessors. A perusal of their contributions will show that Hooker's debt to them, especially to Whitgift, is substantial. Third, his interest in theology and philosophy becomes at times subordinate to his polemic purposes, directed primarily against Puritan opponents, though by no means exclusively so. He accepts the theology of the established church, derived from the Bible and the ancient creeds, expressed in the Book of Common Prayer and the Articles of Religion, though with sufficient ambiguity to permit speculation on minor points of faith. To consider him essentially a philosopher seeking to construct a unified system is to do him a disservice.

The selected bibliography, limited as it is by constraints upon space, has been compiled with some priority given to studies published since the bibliographies of Egil Grislis and W. Speed Hill, with the result that some deserving early works have been omitted. Not the least of problems to the scholar working with Hooker is the matter of finding a suitable text. The standard edition, the seventh of John Keble, is now nearly a century old, and the Folger Library Edition, which provides a superior text, remains incomplete. Since the Folger text will become the standard edition, I have preferred it where possible.

During the course of this study I have received assistance and support from numerous colleges and institutions, and it is a pleasure to acknowledge them. For assistance that was generous, courteous, and at times considerably beyond reasonable expectations, I thank the staffs of the following libraries: the Evans Library of Texas A&M University, The Perry-Castañeda Library of the University of Texas at Austin, the Library of the Victoria College and the University of Houston at Victoria, the Fondren Library of Rice University, and the Bridwell Library, Perkins School of Theology, Southern Methodist University. For help with special problems I am grateful to Ellen S. Dunlap of the Humanities Research Center, the University of Texas, and Patricia Booher, circulation librarian, the Episcopal Theological Library of the Southwest in Austin. Arthur F. Kinney, field editor in charge of Twayne volumes in English literature of the Renaissance, provided valuable guidance on substantive points, and Emily Mc-Keigue, an associate editor at G. K. Hall, gave generous and expert assistance with detailed matters of style and publication.

Among many colleagues at Texas A&M who have been helpful and encouraging, I am especially grateful to Sylvia Grider for assistance in obtaining materials; to David Stewart, who in his role of department head has been supportive in important ways; and to Elizabeth Tebeaux, who shared her scholarly resources and knowledge. I would also like to thank W. David Maxwell, former dean of Liberal Arts at Texas A&M University and now provost at Clemson University, for a College of Liberal Arts research grant during summer, 1980. My greatest debt remains to my wife Mary Lee, who understood, encouraged, and gave cheerful, constant, and able assistance.

Stanley Archer

Texas A&M University

Chronology

1599 *A Christian Letter of Certain English Protestants*, an attack on Hooker's fifth book, published.

1600 November 2, Hooker dies of complications following a chill.

1603 Death of Joan Hooker Nethersole.

1612 Henry Jackson begins publication of Hooker's *Tractates and Sermons*, at the request of John Spenser.

1648 *Of the Laws of Ecclesiastical Polity*, books 6 and 8 published.

1662 *Of the Laws of Ecclesiastical Polity*, book 7, published in the first complete edition, with a biography by John Gauden.

1665 *Life of Richard Hooker* by Izaak Walton published.

Chapter One
Life and Times

The Renaissance in England saw many attempts at intellectual synthesis—impressive and extensive efforts directed toward a kind of comprehensive intellectual unity. Elizabethan England produced men who were inclined to make wide-ranging efforts to draw everything into focus, to reveal and clarify relationships in a fundamentally unified world. One can instance Spenser, seeking to make the Arthurian cycle and chivalry demonstrate the virtues of Renaissance nobility and resolve controversial issues of church and state. Bacon, a far different spirit, took all knowledge as his province and inquired into the questions of how much man knew and how he knew it. It remained for Milton to tell, as no other man had before, the story of all things—to ask and to answer all of the really important questions.

This tendency toward synthesis, so characteristic of the age, manifests itself in the work of Richard Hooker. In his treatise *Of the Laws of Ecclesiastical Polity* he sought, through a synthesis involving philosophy, theology, and law, to provide a reasoned justification of the form, rites, and ceremonies of the Church of England. It was a vast undertaking, running to eight books, three of which remained unpublished until long after the author's death. Yet the work stands among the most impressive and influential intellectual achievements of the English Renaissance.

It is no more possible to account for Hooker's achievement than for those of Shakespeare and Milton, Spenser and Bacon. The little that is known about his background suggests a degree of influence from his associates and from the religious and philosophical currents of his time. Perhaps more than any other, the kind of mind that synthesizes on a grand scale is awakened during periods of intellectual ferment and turbulence.

Early Life

Richard Hooker was born during late March 1554, in or near the city of Exeter, in Devonshire. Izaak Walton, his most important

biographer to date, places his birth in Heavitree, a village suburban
to Exeter.[1] Located along the river Exe near the Cornwall-Devon-
shire border about seventy miles west-southwest of London, Exeter
was at the time of Hooker's birth an important trade center. Its ornate
cathedral was the seat of a bishopric that extended over the two
counties, and it was blessed with a quality grammar school. Five
years before Hooker's birth the city had successfully held out against
a siege by rebellious Catholics and had retained its loyalty to King
Edward VI. The city's importance as a trade center increased in
1564 through the completion of a channel which enabled it to establish a port for merchant ships.

It appears that Hooker's family were of Welsh descent, for the
family surname had originally been Vowell, with a gradual change
to Hooker having begun during the fifteenth century. The family had
produced men of eminence before Hooker's birth. John Hooker, his
great-grandfather, had served as mayor of Exeter in 1490, and his
grandfather Roger held the same office in 1529. An uncle who figures
importantly in his life, another John Hooker, served as chamberlain
of Exeter in 1555 and later represented the city in Parliament.[2] A
student of the law who had traveled widely, he attained eminence
as an antiquary by contributing the annals of Ireland to Raphael
Holinshed's *Chronicles* and through other historical writings on Exeter and Ireland. He had acquired firsthand knowledge of Ireland
through service there under Sir Peter Carew, a native of Exeter, who
held extensive Irish land claims.

About the theologian's father, Roger Hooker, the available information is slight; he appears to have had little association with his
illustrious son. He served under Sir Thomas Chaloner, Tudor statesman, diplomat, soldier, and landowner, and later, as a result of his
brother John's influence, under Sir Peter Carew—an assignment which
took him to Ireland. An extant letter from Roger Hooker to the
Lord Chancellor, dated from Ireland, 10 August 1569, requests the
dispatch of fifty soldiers to repel Irish rebels from a royal household
at Leighlen.[3] Though not an ordained clergyman, Roger became
dean of Leighlen in 1580 and died in Ireland in 1591.

In the absence of his father, Hooker found other friends and
patrons who nurtured his talent and did what they could to advance
his career. Many of those associated with him were bound by similar origins in Devonshire or western England, or by ties of kinship
and marriage. At critical times, there appeared always to be some-

one who would exert influence on his behalf. Never one to sway large numbers as a public figure or to attract a large following, he nonetheless earned the confidence and obtained the support of relatives, friends, and patrons throughout his lifetime. None of those who befriended him turned against him subsequently, and those who favored him with their friendship and support were, more often than not, men of considerable intellectual attainment.

Hooker attended grammar school in his native Exeter, where, according to Walton, he evinced a spirit of inquiry and "a remarkable modesty, and a sweet serene quietness of nature; and ... a quick apprehension of many perplext parts of learning imposed then upon him as a scholar ..." (1:7). The schoolmaster encouraged Hooker's parents to keep him in school and, according to Walton, sought the help of John Hooker to further his nephew's education. Walton believes that John Hooker in turn sought the aid of John Jewel, bishop of Salisbury, to help secure Hooker a place at Corpus Christi College and that the bishop summoned the youth, then fourteen or fifteen, for an interview: "after some questions and observations of the boy's learning, and gravity, and behaviour, the bishop gave his schoolmaster a reward, and took order for an annual pension for the boy's parents, promising also to take him into his care for a future preferment ..." (1:10).

Jewel had written the first important work of religious prose in defense of the Elizabethan Church, *Apologia Ecclesiae Anglicanae* (1562), translated by Lady Ann Bacon as *An Apology of the Church of England.* Though it was written chiefly to answer Catholic polemics, it portrayed the Church of England as a *via media,* a middle way between the extremes of Catholicism and Protestantism, a stance later adopted by Hooker. Jewel may have been influenced in his position by Luther's *Commentary on St. Paul's Book of the Galatians,* in which Luther defended his movement as a moderate course between Catholics and Anabaptists. Jewel's book became one of the most influential documents of the Elizabethan Church, ranking with the Bishops' Bible, the *Book of Common Prayer,* and the *Book of Homilies.*

Oxford

According to Walton, Hooker entered Corpus Christi College, Oxford, during his fifteenth year, most likely during 1568, the year

when William Cole became president of the College. Like many
of Hooker's early benefactors, Cole had been a Marian exile and he
had studied under the theologian Peter Martyr Vermigli. Walton
believes that Cole appointed Hooker a clerk and assigned John
Rainolds as his tutor. Rainolds, from the village of Pinhoe in Devonshire, had entered the college only five years earlier. A man who distinguished himself as a Greek scholar, a rhetorician, and a theologian,
he later became president of the College. When James I came to the
throne Rainolds advised the king to sponsor a new English translation of the Bible, though he did not live to see the completion of
the project he had proposed.

In 1573, when he was nearly twenty, Hooker was designated a
"scholar" or "disciple" of the college on the foundation of the
county of Southampton and was awarded the B.A. degree.[4] He
received the M.A. in 1577 and was designated full fellow in 1579.

Throughout Hooker's twelve years at Oxford, his father served in
Ireland, and the youth seems to have relied upon Cole, his uncle, and
Bishop Jewel for support. Records of the college show that he received at least five grants from a legacy bestowed on the college by
the wealthy London merchant Robert Nowell, a fund established for
the benefit of poor students and at the disposal of Dr. Cole, and it
is possible that he received some support from his native city while
at Oxford.[5] After the death of Bishop Jewel in 1571, he supported
himself in part through tutoring. In about 1573, he became tutor to
Edwin Sandys, son of the bishop of London (later archbishop of
York), and to George Cranmer, a great-nephew of the famous Archbishop Thomas Cranmer. Both pupils became his friends for life.

During Hooker's years at the college, the intellectual currents were
vigorous and diverse. Corpus Christi had been founded by Richard
Foxe in 1515–16, at a time when humanism exerted its greatest
influence on education. The college curriculum stressed Greek and
the works of the ante-Nicene fathers of the church. In his history of
Corpus Christi, Fowler points out that the Catholic influence was
strong down through the reign of Elizabeth, though the reformed
religion prevailed.[6] When Dr. Cole was appointed president, it had
been necessary for him to batter down the doors, which had been
locked against him by those who favored a Catholic.

Of the men who most influenced Hooker at Oxford, several—John
Hooker, William Cole, John Jewel, and Bishop Edwin Sandys—had
been in Europe during the last half of Queen Mary's reign. They were

all moderate reformers, associated in some way with the Protestants at Frankfurt under Richard Cox, who had successfully defended the Second Prayer Book of King Edward VI against the "Knoxians," the Presbyterian followers of John Knox. All had visited Strasbourg where they came under the influence of the theologian Peter Martyr. Hooker's students, Sandys and Cranmer, appeared to represent the central tendencies of the Church of England, as did his friend, fellow student, and later literary executor, John Spenser, yet Hooker's tutor Rainolds recommended the theology of Calvin above all others. In such a varied environment Hooker could not have failed to perceive the usefulness of accommodating diverse theological views; at the same time, that diversity would have stimulated his probing, questioning intellect.

The year 1579 was most unusual for him, for during July he was appointed by the chancellor of Oxford, the earl of Leicester, to deliver the university's Hebrew lecture, owing to the illness of Dr. Thomas Kingsmill, Regius Professor of Hebrew. Hooker retained this responsibility until he left the university, probably in 1584. This appointment suggests intellectual and linguistic accomplishments of a high order.

The year 1579 brought adversity as well as acclaim, for in October, Dr. John Barfoot, the vice-president of the college, expelled Hooker, Rainolds, and several other members for reasons not entirely clear. Barfoot appears at the time to have entertained hopes of succeeding Cole as president, and he later acquired a reputation for dealing sternly with Puritans. In a letter to Sir Francis Knollys about this incident, Rainolds protests that they were expelled "for doing that which by oath we were bound to do" (1:20). Whatever the reasons for the expulsion, Hooker and the others were reinstated about a month afterward, following a review of the matter by the bishop of Winchester. Before the end of 1581, Hooker had taken orders and preached his first public sermon at St. Paul's Cross in London.

Of his personal life and the development of his character at Oxford little information remains that can be reported with assurance. Relying upon tradition, on scattered oral reports, and perhaps upon his own fertile imagination, Walton reported in some detail on Hooker's personal life at college. What he says is consistent with what was known about Hooker at the time and with the man he became. At about age eighteen, Walton reports, he "fell into a dangerous sickness, which lasted two months" (1:12). Upon recovery, he took a

walking trip to Exeter to visit his mother, stopping at Salisbury to
visit with his patron Bishop Jewel, who gave him a walking staff
and a gift of money for himself and his mother. Returning to Salisbury on his trip back to Oxford, he learned of Bishop Jewel's death.
At a loss for support he was reassured by Cole, who provided for
him until some nine months later. By Walton's report, Edwin Sandys,
following a conversation with Bishop Jewel, concluded that Hooker,
then only eighteen years old, should tutor his son. Walton names
Hooker's friends at college as Henry Saville, John Rainolds, and John
Spenser.

One fellow whom Walton did not list, Nicholas Morice, left an
observation of Hooker during his college life. The text was discovered
and translated from the Latin by Ronald Bayne. A student having
delivered a foolish speech at college, Morice observed that if Rainolds
had heard it he "would have averted his eyes at many parts; if Hooker,
he would have smiled, with bent head."[7] This account from a contemporary reflects Hooker's reticence and modesty, which Walton
recognized, but also his sense of humor, which Walton overlooked.
Walton characterizes Hooker's learning at Oxford as follows:

[He] had by a constant unwearied diligence attained unto a perfection in
all the learned languages; by the help of which, an excellent tutor, and his
unintermitted studies, he had made the subtilty of all the arts easy and
familiar to him, and useful for the discovery of such learning as lay hid
from common searchers; so that by these added to his great reason, and
his industry added to both, he did not only know more of causes and
effects; but what he knew, he knew better than other men. (1:14)

Elsewhere in the biography Walton returns to the theme of
Hooker's learning and attributes to him words that seem characteristic, yet like many of Walton's quotations this one has no definite
origin. After Cranmer and Sandys left the college, he writes, Hooker

was daily more assiduous [in his studies]: still enriching his quiet and
capacious soul with the precious learning of the philosophers, casuists, and
schoolmen; and with them, the foundation and reason of all laws, both
sacred and civil. . . . And as he was diligent in these, so he seemed restless
in searching the scope and intention of God's Spirit revealed to mankind
in the sacred scripture. . . . And the good man would often say, that "God
abhors confusion as contrary to his nature;" and as often say, that "the

scripture was not writ to beget disputations and pride, and opposition to government; but moderation, charity, and humility, obedience to authority, and peace to mankind: of which virtues," he would as often say, "no man did ever repent himself upon his death-bed." (1:18–19)

As for his behavior toward others, Walton reports as follows:

it is observable that he was never known to be angry, or passionate, or extreme in any of his desires; never heard to repine or dispute with Providence, but, by a quiet gentle submission and resignation of his will to the wisdom of his Creator, bore the burthen of the day with patience; never heard to utter an uncomely word; and by this, and a grave behaviour, which is a divine charm, he begot an early reverence unto his person, even from those that at other times, and in other companies, took a liberty to cast off that strictness of behaviour and discourse that is required in a collegiate life. (1:15)

Walton adds that in four years he missed the college chapel prayers only twice, and as if to support the testimony of Morice, that "when he took any liberty to be pleasant, his wit was never blemished with scoffing, or the utterance of any conceit that bordered upon, or might beget a thought of looseness in his hearers" (1:15). While Walton wrote in hagiographic tones and revered Hooker as he did the subjects of his other biographies, his words are worthy of some credence, for the portrait of Hooker that he created is one which a study of Hooker's writings renders plausible.

Early Ministry

By 1581, when he was invited by John Aylmer, bishop of London, to deliver the sermon at St. Paul's Cross, a traditional one for young ministers, Hooker had taken orders in the Church of England. The cross stood on the grounds of the cathedral, the one where Hooker preached having been erected during the reign of Henry VII. According to Walton, this assignment first brought Hooker to the house of the affluent London merchant, John Churchman, in Watling Street near the cathedral. For Churchman's home Walton uses the term "Shunamite's House," meaning a lodging provided the preacher for two days prior to the sermon and a day afterward. Although Walton may well be accurate on this point, C. J. Sisson has shown that he is inaccurate in much else regarding the visit to London in 1581.[8] Walton records that Hooker suffered a brief illness while with the Churchmans and that he was nursed back to health by Churchman's wife Alice, who convinced him that with his delicate constitution he needed a wife. When the naive and inexperienced Hooker permitted her to select for him, she selected her daughter Joan, whom Hooker married a year later, a woman with neither "beauty nor portion" 1:24). Hooker may well have stayed in Churchman's house, and he did marry Joan, not in 1582, but six years later in 1588.

In the Paul's Cross sermon, Hooker chose to deal with the doctrine of predestination. The position he defended represented a moderate view of Calvin's doctrine, a view closely in accord with what the Puritans later came to call "Arminianism"—that God has two wills, an antecedent and a consequent will. His antecedent will is that all mankind should be saved, but a second will decrees "that those only should be saved, that did live answerable to that degree of grace which he had offered, or afforded them" (1:22–23), a position Hooker defended throughout his life.

On 9 December 1584, Hooker was appointed vicar of St. Mary's at Drayton-Beauchamp in Buckinghamshire by John Cheny, then patron of the parish. The location was near Aylesbury, about twenty-five miles from Oxford. It is likely that he held this position for only three months, for he was appointed master of the Temple on 17 March 1585. To account for this second appointment Walton gives an anecdote concerning a visit to Drayton-Beauchamp by Sandys and Cranmer, Hooker's former pupils, who supposedly found Hooker reading Horace while tending sheep. When they accompanied him to his house, his wife called him away to rock the cradle. So discouraged were they by the plight of their tutor that they left the following morning, and Sandys later interceded with his father, then the archbishop of York, to obtain for Hooker a more suitable assignment (1:25–26). The anecdote has become well known because of its poignancy, and it contains a kernel of truth, for Sandys did have a role in Hooker's appointment to the Temple. Yet Hooker was unmarried at this time, and it is not clear that he ever resided at Drayton-Beauchamp. It is more likely that he remained in residence at Oxford until he moved to London following his appointment to the Temple, for he considered attendance at a university a valid reason for waiving the rule requiring that priests reside in their parishes.

Master of the Temple

Hooker received royal letters patent appointing him master of the Temple church in London on 17 March 1585, an assignment that brought him firsthand experience in the controversy with the Puritans. The controversy was of long standing, but it had begun in earnest in 1572, with the anonymous publication of "Admonition to the Parliament" seeking drastic reforms within the church. This Admonition Controversy ended in 1577 without any of the Puritan requests being met, but it produced a series of polemic works by Thomas Cartwright on the Puritan side and John Whitgift on the Anglican. Though the Puritans had been thwarted in their efforts at reform, they did not consider their cause lost, as Hooker found when he came to the Temple. The difficulties of this controversy prompted him to begin the great work that would bring forth all his powers, require his attention for the remainder of his life, and establish his place as an author.

The immediate background of the appointment was such that anyone might have predicted adversity for him, but Hooker could not have foreseen what developed. The Temple church was set apart for use by students of the Inner and Middle Temples, law schools whose origin dated from the time of the Knights Templars. Since the reign of Edward III they had been used by students of the common law of England.[9] The church had retained some of its ancient autonomy: the master did not serve under a designated bishop. Though he was provided with living quarters within the Temple, he held no disciplinary authority over the benchers. The government of Elizabeth regarded the position as politically sensitive, since the master's congregation included future lawyers and officers of the law of the realm.

The post fell vacant in August 1584 with the death of Dr. Richard Alvey, who had been in residence since 1560. Walton describes Alvey as an aged and grave man, of deep piety, but one of Puritan leanings. Having grown infirm toward the end of his life, he had been granted the services of a reader to assist with the duties of his office. In 1581 John Aylmer, bishop of London, had appointed as Alvey's assistant Walter Travers, with Thomas Cartwright one of the two most important Puritan intellectuals in England. A rigid and uncompromising Puritan, Travers had not been ordained at the hands of an

English bishop but by a group of protestant ministers at Antwerp, where for a time he had carried on a troubled ministry. Upon returning to England, he became chaplain to William Cecil, Lord Burghley, and Cecil interceded with Aylmer to secure his assignment to the Temple.

As a reader and de facto master Travers carried out his duties with energy and enthusiasm. He also found additional time and energy to further the cause of Puritanism through his writings. For an anti-Catholic tract published in 1583 he received recognition from the government. With Cartwright, Travers agreed that the presbyterian system of church government was not merely in accord with the New Testament, but that it was the only legitimate system. In the face of the queen's opposition to Presbyterianism and her determination to promote uniformity of worship in England, Travers gained no ground. At the Temple he was the obvious choice to succeed Alvey, but he was denied the position for two reasons.

First, in his position as subordinate to Alvey, Travers had made unpopular innovations that had to be revoked because they had offended some of the benchers. He had attempted to change the communion service so that the communicants neither kneeled nor sat, but stood, a practice for which he found precedent at Zurich. The benchers objected and returned to their customary practice of sitting, as had been done at the Last Supper.[10] He had also appointed among the congregation collectors to distribute contributions to the poor and side men to observe slackness in divine duties and report offenders to the master for admonition. By ancient custom and practice ministers at the Temple held no disciplinary power over the congregation, and Travers's innovation, though approved by the Privy Council beforehand, was to the benchers unpopular and unacceptable.

The second reason for denying Travers the post was more formidable than the opinions of the benchers, for he faced the determined opposition of John Whitgift, archbishop of Canterbury (1583–1604). Courageous, resolute, persistent, and endowed with an iron will, Whitgift had been chosen by the queen to succeed the weak and ineffectual Edmund Grindal, and he usually enjoyed the unwavering support of the queen. Though he had no official authority over the appointment to the Temple, the archbishop pointed out to the queen by letter that the audience included many who would hold positions of importance in future years and that "the said Travers hath been and is one of the chief and principal authors of dissension in this church, a contemner of the book of Prayers, and of other orders by authority established; an earnest seeker of innovation; either in no degree of the ministry at all, or else ordered beyond the seas..." (1:29). Whitgift knew that Travers had the powerful support of Cecil, yet he opposed the appointment and recommended, tactfully enough, one of the queen's chaplains, Dr. Bond. Concerning this recommendation, Cecil informed the archbishop that Travers was the choice of Alvey and "a number of honest gentlemen of the Temple" and that the queen thought Dr. Bond unsuitable "because of his infirmities" (1:30). The matter remained unresolved for several months until Archbishop Sandys, the father of Hooker's pupil, put forward Hooker's name and secured the queen's approval.

With this as background, the new master would inevitably find the position uncomfortable. Travers and Hooker had family ties, Travers's brother John, also a clergyman, having married Hooker's cousin; by way of further complication, Travers kept his position as reader and remained in residence at the Temple. It was arranged that Hooker would deliver the morning sermon while Travers would preach in the afternoon; as Thomas Fuller put it, "The pulpit spake pure Canterbury in the morning, and Geneva in the afternoon."[11] Not only did Hooker endure doctrinal opposition from his subordinate; he found himself pitted against one who preached more effectively than he, at least according to Fuller: "*Mr Hooker* his voice was low, stature little, gesture none at all, standing stone-still in the Pulpit, as if the posture of his body were the emblem of his minde, unmoveable in his opinions. Where his eye was left fixed at the beginning, it was found fixed at the end of his Sermon.... His style was long and pithy, driving a whole flock of several *Clauses* before he came to the *Close* of a sentence."[12] Travers, on the other hand, preached with skill and with telling effect: "*Mr Travers* his utterance was gracefull, matter profitable, method plain, and his style carried in it *indolem pietatis a Genius of grace* flowing from his sanctified heart."[13]

Hooker's difficulty began even before he delivered his first sermon, when Travers asked him to delay it until the master was presented by him to the congregation. According to Hooker's later explanation,

the evening before I was first to preach, he came, and two other **gentlemen** joined with him in the charge of this church, (for so he gave me to under-

stand,) though not in the same kind of charge with him: the effect of
his conference then was, that he thought it his duty to advise me not to
enter with a strong hand, but to change my purpose of preaching there
the next day, and to stay till he had given notice of me to the congregation, that so their allowance might seal my calling. (3:571)

To this Hooker responded that the ecclesiastical order implied by
Travers's request did not exist in the Temple and that he could not
accept it.

Within the next few months the controversy generated by two
strongly opposed points of view broke into the open. Matters reached
a head almost exactly a year after Hooker's appointment, and the
controversy was brought to a sudden end when Travers was silenced
by order of the archbishop of Canterbury. From Travers's point of
view, Hooker had erred in placing too much emphasis upon private
reason and the evidence of the senses and in making too liberal an
interpretation of predestination. He had counseled with the master
in private on these questions and, not succeeding in reaching an
agreement, had challenged his superior from the pulpit, contrary to
canon law. In March 1586 Hooker delivered a series of three sermons on salvation and justification, and in his afternoon sermon
Travers answered some points raised by each. The first sermon was
typically irenic, showing similarities between the Church of England
and the Roman Catholic church. In a fiercely anti-Catholic time in
English history, Hooker argued that under limited conditions even a
papist might be saved.

His second sermon dealt with a text in Galatians and with the
question of priorities between faith and works. Travers's biographer
gives the following account of his reply: "Travers did not have time
for a private talk with his opponent, but nevertheless, having delivered
his afternoon sermon, he decided to add a short speech denouncing
Hooker's views. This act he justified as following the example of
Paul...."[14] Within two weeks the archbishop had prepared and sent
a letter silencing Travers, an order which remained in effect for the
remainder of Travers's life. According to Fuller, it arrived just as
Travers was approaching the pulpit to deliver yet another sermon.[15]

Travers appealed his case in *A Supplication Made to the Privy
Council*, a manuscript pamphlet that was copied and widely circulated at the time. His appeal was answered by Hooker in an address
to the archbishop, *The Answere of Mr. Richard Hooker* (first pub-

lished in 1612). Both pamphlets were moderate, even respectful in tone; Hooker and Travers apparently retained respect for each other throughout their trying controversy. Travers's appeal to the Privy Council failed, and the pamphlets ended the controversy between the two men.

There is no reason to believe that Hooker sought the intercession of the archbishop, and, after silencing Travers, Whitgift gave little attention to their controversy. Had he given unstinting support to Hooker, he might have appeared to be favoring one who had defended Catholicism. Yet after this time the guiding influence of Whitgift is often to be observed in Hooker's life. For Travers the result was less fortunate. Before he could be given another assignment, the archbishop insisted, he was required to be properly ordained by an English bishop, a step that he was unwilling to take. It might be noted that on similar grounds, failure to accept proper ordination, Whitgift had dismissed Thomas Cartwright from his fellowship at Cambridge. Travers lived in his quarters in the Temple for a few months and then became provost of Trinity College, Dublin. He lived until 1636, and the last work from his pen was a defense of the Church of England against recusants.[16] Hooker continued his ministry at the Temple until 1591, when he was appointed by Whitgift to the parish of Boscombe, near Salisbury, in Wiltshire.

Marriage

Except for a few names and details about offspring, most accounts of Hooker's marriage have been misleading, until C. J. Sisson cleared up many of the misconceptions in his *The Judicious Marriage of Mr. Hooker* (1940). Thomas Fuller, John Gauden, Izaak Walton, and Anthony Wood had misjudged and misinterpreted the facts, and biographers continued to repeat the earlier accounts, almost all tending to support the view that Joan Churchman was an unsuitable wife.

In his thorough study of the question, Sisson concluded that Hooker lived in London at the home of his father-in-law John Churchman from 1584 until 1591. Churchman's house in Watling Street was near St. Paul's and only a quarter mile from the Temple. Churchman's son William was a student at Corpus Christi College, where Hooker may have known him.

He married Joan Churchman, according to parish records at the Church of St. Augustine's, on 13 February 1588. As to his residence after marriage, Sisson concludes: "It seems reasonably certain that, after his appointment to the Mastership, and also after his marriage, Hooker continued to live, with his wife and his growing family, in Churchman's house."[17] His father-in-law's home seems also to have been a gathering place for his friends. Edwin Sandys lived with the Churchman family for approximately five years, apparently paying no rent.

John Churchman was a wealthy and respected London merchant who became master of the Merchant Taylors Company in 1594. Far from marrying into a penniless household, as Walton led readers to believe, Hooker married into one of affluence, and his wife brought him a substantial dowry.[18] Records of the Merchant Taylors Company and legal records of suits following the deaths of Hooker and his wife, minutely examined by Sisson, permit no other conclusion. Evidence of closeness between Hooker and his in-laws is cogent. His sons Richard (b. 1589) and Edwin (b. 1596) and his daughters Alice (b. 1590) and Cecily (b. 1591) were christened in St. Augustine's Church, the home parish of the Churchman family. His daughter Jane was baptized at St. Andrews, Enfield, in 1592. Enfield, where John Churchman had an estate, was also the burial place for Hooker's two young sons.

After painstaking examination of the evidence, Sisson reached the following conclusion about Hooker's marriage: "His marriage was beyond question judicious, and we may believe that it was happy. It gave him an assured position, not only as the Master of the Temple, the friend of Edwin Sandys, and one in favour at Canterbury, but also as a member of the family circle of a great London citizen of wealth and civic rank. And his wife's dowry provided financial security for himself and his children."[19] Although Sisson provides no documentation to substantiate the dowry provided Joan by her father, a generous amount seems the most likely explanation for Hooker's sizable estate at his death, despite Walton's praise of Hooker's servant Thomas Lane for his financial shrewdness.

Boscombe and *Ecclesiastical Polity*

Hooker probably began his great defense of the Church of England while living at the home of John Churchman and serving as master of the Temple. There is no record of the instant in his life when he was prompted to begin writing *Of the Laws of Ecclesiastical Polity*, nothing analogous to Gibbon's hearing the barefoot friars singing hymns in the Temple of Jupiter and having the thought of writing a history of the empire start into his mind. Hooker's experience with Travers may well have prompted him to explore the broad issues of religious controversy and to begin work on his great treatise. Keble believed that Hooker began his work in 1586, when he was still at the Temple, a plausible suggestion since the form and approach may have been influenced by the author's experience among lawyers and students of the law. Recently, Rudolph Almasy has developed the view that Hooker may have begun his treatise as an answer to Cartwright's *Second Reply* (1577), written during the Admonition Controversy with Whitgift and left unanswered.[20]

Three years after the author's death, his friend John Spenser, who had known Hooker since their days at Corpus Christi College, recorded his version of what influenced Hooker to begin his work:

So much better were it in those our dwellings of peace, to endure any inconvenience whatsoever in the outward frame, than in desire of alteration, thus to set the whole house on fire. Which moved the religious heart of this learned writer, in zeal of God's truth, and in compassion to his church, the mother of us all,... to stand up and take upon him a general defence both of herself, and of her established laws; and by force of demonstration, so far as the nature of the present matter could bear, to make known to the world and these oppugners of her, that all those bitter accusations laid to her charge, are not the faults of her laws and orders, but either their own mistakes in the misunderstanding, or the abuses of men in the ill execution of them. (1:121–22)

Spenser seems to sense in Hooker's resistance to change, indicative of his basically conservative temperament, a reason for his writing his treatise.

Whitgift seems deliberately to have chosen for Hooker a parish assignment that would enable him to carry on his work, an assignment which Walton would have us believe Hooker requested. He became rector of Boscombe, prebend of Netheravon, and subdean of Sarum, appointments made by Whitgift since the bishopric of Salisbury was vacant at the time. Dr. Nicholas Baldgay, who previously held the modest livings which Hooker received, replaced Hooker at the Temple. It appears that Hooker was a nonresident, or that he resided in his parish only a part of the time, while he spent most of his time at his father-in-law's home in London. Four books

of *Ecclesiastical Polity*, representing about one third of the entire
work, were entered in the Stationer's Register in January 1593 and
were published later that year.

It might be supposed that the church and government which Hooker
had labored with such care to defend would have sponsored the publication and rewarded him for his work. Nothing could be further
from the truth. The author himself sought to interest printers in the
work and met with discouraging refusals on the grounds that works
of religious controversy did not sell. Only the effort of Hooker's friend
and former pupil Edwin Sandys, then a member of Parliament, who
assumed financial responsibility for the project, assured publication
of the first five books of Hooker's treatise. After examining the records of Hooker's arrangement with Sandys, Sisson concluded that
Sandys spent 267 pounds for the publication of the five books.[21] Of
this amount Hooker received thirty pounds, the total earnings for
him and his family from his work. It appears that Hooker persuaded
Sandys to sell the volumes as cheaply as possible, and though the
estimated 1,200 copies of books 1–4 were sold within eleven years,
it is unlikely that Sandys recovered expenses before his death in 1629.
The printer and bookseller was John Windet, a Devonshire man
and Hooker's first cousin, who specialized in printing religious books.
The text of *Ecclesiastical Polity* was produced with accuracy of a
high order for its time.

Rector of Bishopsbourne

In July 1595 Hooker became rector of Bishopsbourne, located
only about four miles southeast of Canterbury, under circumstances
which suggest that the appointment was a promotion. His predecessor,
Dr. William Redman, had moved to the bishopric of Norwich, one
of the twenty bishoprics then within the see of Canterbury. The
rector had as his residence a large house of twelve rooms, and the
location was near an important center of power, although the archbishop usually resided at Lambeth. Bishopsbourne is the one parish
in which Hooker is known to have lived, although he appears to have
made frequent trips to London to oversee publication of book 5 of
his treatise, published in 1597.

His principal work during the years between the publication of
book 5 and his death in 1600 must have been on the remaining three
books of his treatise, a task left incomplete. But at Bishopsbourne he

also carried on the active life of a parish priest. He became a friend of Dr. Hadrian Saravia, who had written a defense of the church hierarchy and who had served as Whitgift's chaplain. He knew the names of his parishoners, visited the sick, admonished his people to be peaceable, and maintained in his parish such customs as fasting and walking the parish boundaries during the Rogation Days, customs which had by that time diminished in popularity. He remained modest and somewhat shy; one of Walton's informants reported that Hooker was unwilling to look a man in the face and that he was "of so mild and humble a nature, that his poor parish-clerk and he did never talk but with both their hats on, or both off, at the same time" (1:78). In appearance he was not imposing, "a man in poor clothes, his loins usually girt in a coarse gown, or canonical coat; of a mean stature, and stooping, and yet more lowly in the thoughts of his soul; his body worn out, not with age, but study, and holy mortifications; his face full of heat-pimples, begot by his unactivity and sedentary life" (1:77).

If an anecdote related by Gauden and Walton and referred to by Henry King is correct, a holy life did not secure him from slanderous accusation and extortion by three Puritans, two men and a woman. According to the anecdote they extorted money from him periodically until he told his plight to Sandys and Cranmer. When confronted with the truth by Hooker's friends, they admitted their guilt and repented for the wrong they had done Hooker, who rejoiced to be rid of the burden.

According to Walton, he died after a lingering illness, first manifesting itself as a cold contracted during a passage from London to Gravesend by water. He died on 2 November 1600 at the age of forty-six, after Saravia had administered last rites. He was buried in the chancel of his church at Bishopsbourne, where a monument was erected to his memory by Sir William Cowper in 1635.

Hooker's will, dated 26 October 1600, left each of his four daughters 100 pounds, to be paid at the time of her marriage. The will left the bulk of his estate to Joan Hooker, "my wel beloved wife, whom I ordaine and make sole executor of this my last will and testament" (1:89). It bequeaths money to the poor and sets aside three pounds for rebuilding the pulpit of the church. As overseers he appoints his friend Edwin Sandys and his "wel-beloved father, Mr. John Churchman" (1:89).

His estate at the time of death was valued at 1,092 pounds, most of it in household property and books.[22] His widow remarried within about five months to Edmund Nethersole, a citizen of Canterbury, but died in 1603, survived by her four daughters by Hooker. At Hooker's death books 6–8 of *Ecclesiastical Polity* had not been published, and the manuscripts were, presumably, incomplete at the time. Books 6 and 8 were published in 1648, and book 7 in 1662.

The image of Hooker left to us by Walton is that of a man who, having been nurtured in devotion by his mother, lived the life of a scholarly saint, and this image seems reasonably accurate. Though Walton's view was influenced by the awe and respect he held for his subject, little in the record runs counter to it. There is, however, a kind of general corroboration in the writings of Hooker's contemporaries, for example William Camden, William Covel, and John Spenser. Spenser, writing about four years after Hooker's death, affirms that the impression left in Hooker's writings is authentic:

What admirable height of learning and depth of judgment dwelled in the lowly mind of this true humble man, great in all wise men's eyes, except his own; with what gravity and majesty of speech his tongue and pen uttered heavenly mysteries, whose eyes in the humility of his heart were always cast down to the ground; how all things that proceeded from him were breathed, as from the spirit of love, as if he like the bird of the Holy Ghost, the dove, had wanted gall; let them that knew him not in his person judge by . . . his writings. For out of these, even those who otherwise agree not with him in opinion, do afford him the testimony of a mild and a loving spirit; and of his learning, what greater proof can we have than this, that his writings are most admired by those who themselves do most excel in judicious learning, and by them the more often they are read, the more highly they are extolled and desired? (1:122)

By calling attention to humility, modesty, and learning Spenser emphasized traits that have been attributed to Hooker ever since. The word "judicious," used here in reference to the writings, soon became an epithet with Hooker.

In an age which commonly witnessed extravagant and sometimes outrageous rhetoric in religious controversy, Hooker maintained a restrained tone and dignified style that set him apart. One has only to think of the Marprelate pamphlets and the solemn vituperation of Milton's tracts to realize how far religious polemicists could go when borne on the wings of zeal. Not even Dryden, rationalist though he was, could avoid extremes of tone and language when he felt a serious issue was at stake. Hooker, no less devoted to Christianity, maintained his elevated tone and rarely indulged in sarcasm, ad hominem attacks, or humor at his opponents' expense.

That he elicited and enjoyed the loyalty and esteem of learned men of his day says something important about his learning and his character. The support he received from Jewel, Rainolds, Whitgift, Spenser, Saravia, Sandys, and Cranmer suggests that his merit was recognized. That he was not handsomely rewarded by the church says more about the times than about his friends' devotion to him, though there is no indication that he suffered want or poverty, as John Donne, for example, did.

It was given to men of vision during the Renaissance to plan and design more than they could complete. Hooker's great synthesis, like Spenser's *Faerie Queene* and Bacon's Great Instauration, remained incomplete at his death. Yet he came closer than they to completing his ambitious undertaking, and of the eight books, perhaps only the sixth remains seriously incomplete. He produced the most comprehensive defense of the Elizabethan religious settlement of its time, the culmination of four decades of challenges to the church by Puritans and Catholics. *Ecclesiastical Polity* has been called the first great masterpiece of English prose written by a single author. We turn to Hooker for an account of the theological and a portion of the legal thought of his time, and in its own kind his work is unsurpassed. Of the many apologists for the Church of England during his time, he stands in a line leading from Jewel through Whitgift, and his achievement eclipses those of his predecessors.

Chapter Two
Minor Works

The minor works of Hooker, designated in some editions as *opuscula*, consist of seven sermons, one pamphlet, three letters, and miscellaneous notes and fragments—the sermons and two replies to attacks on him being the most significant. None of these works was published during his lifetime, and some first appeared long after his death.[1] Although the chronology of the Hooker canon has not been fully ascertained, the minor works include his earliest known writings and probably his last work, the fragmentary reply to *A Christian Letter*. At least three of the sermons and one reply, the *Answer to Travers*, were written before *Ecclesiastical Polity* and are seminal—illustrating the range of his intellect and his major themes; consequently, the minor writings will be considered before an analysis of *Ecclesiastical Polity*.

Sermons

Responsibility for editing the sermons fell to Henry Jackson of Corpus Christi College, who saw six of them through the press between 1612 and 1614. A seventh was published by Walton in his biography of Robert Sanderson in 1678.

Because of their extraordinary length and their careful organization, some of the sermons, notably sermons 1–3, can be considered either compilations of a series or tractates. Sermon 2 exceeds twenty thousand words, and sermon 3, published in incomplete form, runs to approximately eighteen thousand. By contrast, sermon 7, found among the papers of Bishop Lancelot Andrews, is about three thousand words long.

The style does not scintillate, as the style of Donne's sermons does, nor does it promote the ease of reading that comes from a command of idiom such as Archbishop John Tillotson possessed. Hooker's metaphors are tame by comparison with Donne's, yet they are typically more effective in promoting understanding. The sentences are unusually long, yet the organization is carefully controlled, frequently through point-by-point analysis supported by wide-ranging references from the Bible and church fathers.

The sermons fall readily into three groups in accordance with their purposes and subjects: sermons 1–3 concern faith and justification; sermon 4, the only funeral sermon, and sermon 7, which treats of prayer, deal with human privation and need; sermons 5–6 assail false prophets and divisions within the church.

Sermons 1–3: Faith and Justification.   Sermon 1, entitled "A Learned and Comfortable Sermon of the Certainty and Perpetuity of Faith in the Elect," is based on the verse from Habakkuk, "Therefore the law is slacked, and judgment doth never go forth" (3:469). Both this one and Hooker's second sermon appear to come from a series on Habakkuk delivered at the Temple in 1585–86. It concerns what was perhaps the single most important topic in the sermons as a whole, the nature of faith. Its main point is to establish whether by perceiving the law to fail Habakkuk was acknowledging a loss of faith. Before coming to analysis of the question, Hooker considers another which, from the wording of his introduction, may have been explored in an earlier sermon no longer extant: "why they that do [believe], do it many times with small assurance" (3:469). To answer the question he distinguishes between "certainty of evidence" and "certainty of adherence" and follows his inclination to mark a distinction between nature and grace: "That which we see by the light of grace, though it be indeed more certain [as an abstract proposition]; yet is it not to us so evidently certain, as that which sense or the light of nature will not suffer a man to doubt of."[2] Since as a result of original sin no human being can have perfect faith, Hooker thinks that doubt should not be equated with disbelief. Even though the degree of faith varies among men and even though perfect faith is unattainable, God gives all believers an adequate faith: "Wherefore he worketh that certainty in all, which sufficeth abundantly to their salvation in the life to come; but in none so great as attaineth in this life unto perfection" (3:472).

As to whether doubt of the law argues a loss of faith, Hooker is unequivocal: "we teach that the faith whereby ye are sanctified cannot fail; it did not in the Prophet, it shall not in you" (3:473). What appears to the believer to be a loss of faith only seems so and in fact his doubt arises from three causes: (1) any comparison which seems to indicate a stronger faith within others or previously within oneself; (2) an expectation that joy always accompanies faith; and

(3) a fear that temptations indicate an absence of faith. But none of these demonstrates a loss of faith, a turning from belief to unbelief: "The faith therefore of true believers, though it have many and grievous downfalls, yet doth it still continue invincible..." (3:476). Sermon 1 is remarkable in Hooker's thought because of his strong emphasis on faith, a position which he never alters, and his inclination to view the order of grace as open to all and to see man throughout life as achieving sanctification through faith.

The second sermon, like the first, is based upon Habakkuk 1:4, and is entitled "A Learned Discourse of Justification, Works, and How the Foundation of Faith is Overthrown." It was probably delivered in late March 1586, during Hooker's controversy with Travers.[3] It is Hooker's longest and most complex sermon, dealing with soteriology, an abstruse topic in religious controversy during the time. In this sermon, in contrast to the first where Hooker concerned himself with personal faith, the subject concerns faith or beliefs within an institution or church. Like the other reformers, Hooker is faced with denying both the legitimacy and the validity of Roman Catholic doctrine, while not denying salvation to all the adherents, past and present, of the church of Rome. The errors of the Roman church had to appear great enough to justify schism, but not so great as to make it appear that all of Western Christendom for hundreds of years preceding the Reformation had been lost. (To the extreme Puritans, the second part of the problem posed no real difficulty, but to most of moderate leanings it did.) Hooker undertakes to explain why he considers the church of Rome an authentic church and to clarify important doctrinal differences between it and the Church of England. He is also concerned with the problem of how those *within* the universal Christian church can determine that members have fallen so far from grace that they are lost.

The first part of the sermon gives a brief account of common beliefs held by Roman and Reformed churches, and then it turns to areas of difference. Hooker makes sweeping denunciations of "heresies" in the Roman church, including positions on two sacraments—penance and the eucharist. But his primary effort is to differentiate beliefs about justification, and in so doing he attacks Roman Catholic doctrine concerning grace—grace within the Christian, its attainment through works and various acts, its diminution through sin, and its enhancement or restoration through sacraments and sacramentals.

While he clearly accepts the reference to Babylon in Revelations

18:4 as prophetic of the Roman church, he argues that some who remain within it may be saved and restates his position on this from the first sermon, expanding it further. Hooker's position turns upon his explanation of the foundation of the Christian faith as it applies to believers before the Reformation: "But as many as hold the foundation which is precious, though they hold it but weakly, and as it were by a slender thread, although they frame many base and unsuitable things upon it, . . . yet shall they pass the fiery trial and be saved, which indeed have builded themselves upon the rock, which is the foundation of the Church" (3:500). Hooker explains this foundation in several ways, some of them from New Testament passages, but all amount to this: "Christ crucified for the salvation of the world" (3:502), that is, faith in Christ as Savior. Those holding additional false beliefs, while accepting the foundation, are like the Galatians, whom Paul condemned for their insistence on the requirement of circumcision because it upheld a legalistic interpretation of salvation.

But Hooker is reluctant to condemn anyone for erroneous beliefs, preferring to think that some of the Galatians were saved despite their error. The same consideration applies to those Christians who have lived and died in the Roman church, though for those who overthrew the foundation of faith, those who taught that salvation is impossible except through works, "their case is dreadful" (3:504). Not all false beliefs deny the foundation of Christianity, and many of the Roman Christians accept some false beliefs of their Church but not others. Still other members may be unable to grasp the full implications of what they believe because of ambiguous wording of those beliefs. Therefore, Hooker concludes, "we may hope that thousands of our fathers living in popish superstitions might be saved" (3:509).

He proceeds to develop another major issue: "What if neither that of the Galatians concerning circumcision, nor this of the church of Rome about works, be any direct denial of the foundation, as it is affirmed that both are?" (3:510). The question does not entirely clarify what Hooker is about here, which is to explain how the Roman church of his time should be regarded by those in his own branch of the church rather than how the fathers and others of that church may have fared previously. Since this subject is more sensitive, his caution is understandable. A five-point outline which he provided for the remainder of his sermon demonstrates Hooker's inclination to organize carefully:

the foundation of faith, direct denial of the foundation, whether the justified may deny it, "whether the Galatians did so," and "whether the church of Rome, for this one opinion of works, may be thought to do the like..." (3:510). Each point is elaborated in detail, and so important to Hooker's soteriology is the sermon that some major parts will be examined.

As one would expect, the entire text is carefully reasoned. To the foundation of salvation through Christ, he attaches a qualification: "we teach plainly, that to hold the foundation is, in express terms to acknowledge it" (3:513–14). To clarify the second major point, what it is to deny the foundation, Hooker identifies two types of denial: direct and indirect. Those who deny Christ outright deny directly; those who hold heretical views whose consequent logical effect is to deny or abrogate the foundation, such as the belief that salvation is achieved through works, deny indirectly. Yet an indirect denial does not deprive them of the name Christian, for in some sense they still subscribe to the foundation (3:515).

As to his third point, whether once having embraced Christianity a soul may fall so far as to deny it, Hooker maintains the strong negative position he established in his first sermon. Some who seem to have fallen, who even believe themselves fallen, "notwithstanding are still alive unto God in Christ" (3:517). Hooker tends to interpret scriptural promises here literally, not as applied to men in general, but to individuals, and his soteriology appears to be highly individualistic. While he does not deny the necessity of repentance, he seems to believe that those who accept the foundation will repent when necessary.

As Hooker's belief applies to heresy, it leaves little chance for a loss of salvation thereby: "I may safely set it down, that if the justified err, as he may, and never come to understand his error, God doth save him through general repentance: but if he fall into heresy, he calleth him either at one time or other by actual repentance; but from infidelity, which is an inward direct denial of the foundation, preserveth him by special providence for ever" (3:520). There is, then, no such thing as lapsing or falling indirectly. If acceptance of the foundation is understood as a positive act of will, then denial must also be considered a positive act, one which to Hooker would hardly be conceivable, though he admits that some of the Galatians, after reproof from Paul, probably denied the foundation.

As for the final point concerning the Roman church, Hooker quotes several reformers, including Calvin, to show that nothing in its theology directly denies the foundation and therefore it is not to be denied designation as a church. Even here, in a sermon on such a controversial matter, Hooker attempts to avoid unfairness: "Let us beware, lest if we make too many ways of denying Christ, we scarce leave any way for ourselves truly and soundly to confess him" (3:528). An analogy between the Galatians and Catholicism on works, according to Hooker's reasoning, does not really apply. The error of the Roman church is that "she attributeth unto works a power of satisfying God for sin; and a virtue to merit both grace here, and in heaven glory" (3:532), which doctrine, though it opposes the foundation of faith, does not deny it indirectly.

In this sermon there is the well-known passage promoting a more tolerant attitude toward Catholicism than had been uttered publicly in England for many years:

Give me a man, of what estate or condition soever, yea, a cardinal or a pope, whom at the extreme point of his life affliction hath made to know himself; whose heart God hath touched with true sorrow for all his sins, and filled with love toward the Gospel of Christ; whose eyes are opened to see the truth, and his mouth to renounce all heresy and error any way opposite thereunto, this one opinion of merits excepted; which he thinketh God will require at his hands, and because he wanteth, therefore, trembleth, and is discouraged; ... shall I think, because of this only error, that such a man toucheth not so much as the hem of Christ's garment? (3:541)

As he does elsewhere, Hooker demonstrates a tolerant, irenist attitude, and he admonishes his auditors not to be quick to assume that others have missed salvation. His Christian perspective requires the belief that salvation is open to those of other national churches, even when their beliefs are perceived as false.

Sermon 3, "A Learned Sermon of the Nature of Pride," also based on a verse from Habakkuk (2:4), was published in an incomplete text in 1612. Of all of Hooker's sermons, this one best reflects the majestic sweep of intellect that would later produce *Of the Laws of Ecclesiastical Polity*. Though its title suggests a major emphasis upon pride, the sermon emphasizes faith and represents an important statement of Hooker's soteriology.

He begins not with pride but with law, making the point that even the law of God is more willingly obeyed when men understand the need for it. His reason for stressing this is not entirely clear unless he believes that the prophet's meaning is thereby expressed. He gives an account of why the Babylonian king's mind is swollen, and so lays a groundwork which clarifies the necessity for law and illustrates the Aristotelian basis of Hooker's thought:

All things which God did create, he made them at the first true, good, and right: true, in respect of correspondence unto that pattern of their being, which was eternally drawn in the counsel of God's foreknowledge; good, in regard of the use and benefit which each thing yieldeth unto other; right, by an apt conformity of all parts with that end which is outwardly proposed for each thing to tend unto. Other things have ends proposed, but have not the faculty to know, judge, and esteem of them. . . . Only men in all their actions know what it is which they seek for, neither are they by any such necessity tied naturally unto any determinate mean to obtain their end by, but that they may, if they will, forsake it. (3:598–99)

In Hooker's teleological view, man's end is the happiness of immortality, and among men the difference between "right and crooked minds, is in the means which the one or the other do eschew or follow" (3:599). Things of the world are necessary to man, Hooker acknowledges, but man's quest of all things must be governed by law: "His mind is perverse, kam, and crooked, not when it bendeth itself unto any of these things, but when it bendeth so, that it swerveth either to the right hand or to the left, by excess or defect, from that exact rule whereby human actions are measured. The rule to measure and judge them by, is the law of God" (3:599–600). In a tremendous linkage, whose implications are far-reaching, he gives a definition of law which follows Thomas Aquinas and rests heavily upon Paul in Romans 2:14–15: "Under the name of the Law, we must comprehend not only that which God hath written in tables and leaves, but that which nature hath engraven in the hearts of men" (3:600). The law of nature guides the pagan, and its violation convicts the Babylonian monarch.

But the Babylonian king is not alone, and Hooker's explanation of this foreshadows his long discussion of faith and salvation in this sermon. Because no man can adequately follow the law, the failure to obey may lead to despair. But law is given to man so that he may recognize his inability to follow its directives and therefore may come to believe that something greater is necessary: "Here cometh necessarily in a new way unto salvation, so that they which were in the other perverse, may in this be found straight and righteous. That the way of nature, this the way of grace. . . . the end of this way, salvation bestowed upon men as a gift, presupposing, not their righteousness, but the forgiveness of their unrighteousness, justification; their justification, not their natural ability to do good, but their hearty sorrow for not doing, and unfeigned belief in Him . . ." (3:600–601). Failure to distinguish clearly between nature and grace, Hooker says, has given rise to great confusion both in the church and within the souls of men.

The sermon proceeds to examine the nature of pride, its dangers, its effects, and its cure. Pride, which Hooker finds leads to other extremes, is best cured by the "rod of divine chastisement." Before ending his first section he turns to an analysis and explication of "the just by his faith shall live," giving attention first to the meaning of *live*.

In the remainder of the sermon, Hooker considers the nature of justice—in general, in God, and in the lives of men. To explain justice in general he depends heavily upon the meaning of law. Man's inclination toward justice grows out of a principle of nature: "So hath that supreme commander disposed it, that each creature should have some peculiar task and charge, reaching furder than only unto its own preservation" (3:617). This principle applies to men, who have mutual duties toward others. Hooker extends this obligation to an impressive degree: "although the want of any [man] be a token of some defect in that mutual assistance which should be; yet howsoever to have such want supplied were far from equity and justice. If it be so, then must we find out some rule which determineth what every one's due is, from whom, and how, it must be had" (3:618). Justice, then, is defined by law, either by natural law, which is immutable, or by postitive law, which is subject to change. He goes on to make a clear point about positive law; even positive laws instituted by God may be subject to change, as the Bible clearly demonstrates.

Though he distinguishes the three kinds of justice—distributive, commutative, and corrective—he does not dwell upon each at length. Rather he admonishes his hearers not to be too quick to conclude that injustice has been done or to take offense at injustice, since even the wisest men find justice difficult to asertain and to achieve.

In the third section Hooker analyzes the justice of God, and one portion foreshadows his conception that God operates according to law. Divine nature is just because it is good, Hooker argues, but in postulating a divine law he makes use of the tentative tone of the rhetorical question: "Then seeing God doth work nothing but for some end, which end is the cause of that he doth, what letteth to conclude that God doth all things even in such sort as law prescribeth?" (3:626). The conception of a just Deity is reassuring, even though Hooker would recognize that divine law reaches beyond man's intellectual capacity. The qualities of Deity which Hooker chooses to stress are those of consistency, reasonableness, and justice—not mysteriousness, inscrutability, and arbitrariness, a view of God's nature which places him in opposition to most Puritans and allies him with St. Thomas.

After showing what many biblical passages reveal about God's justice, Hooker turns to a matter that appears to indicate a defect of divine justice—the problem of the prosperity of sin in the world. He undertakes a long examination of distributive justice, its merit in rewarding each man according to his deserts, man's desire for it, God's words that support it, and the generally beneficial effects it would have among men. He points out, though, that the rule of distributive justice cannot be applied to man's earthly existence alone, giving numerous examples (chiefly from the life of Christ) to show that the most meritorious beings on earth did not have the most comfortable lives. Early martyrs of the church would not have changed place with the pope, Hooker says, in another aside against Rome. Apparent evil is only that, and "the rule of distributive justice is not violated" (3:634). Good fortune in the world comes to those for whom it is a real good: "The life of the just shall be long and fortunate; they shall see many and happy days; their prosperity is a sequel of their piety; but with exception, unless it be far better for them to be otherwise" (3:635). Mistakes about distributive justice occur when men take too shallow a view of the questions raised by it.

Sermon 3 closes with a discussion of the point of view which demands that corrective justice be satisfied after God has forgiven man, "till transgressors have endured, either in this world or another, vexation proportionable unto the pleasure which they have taken in doing evil..." (3:637), or, in other words, a belief in purgatory. He gives a lengthy and seemingly impartial account of belief in punishment after death short of hell, and the sermon ends at the point where his refutation of the Catholic position was to have begun.

Sermons 4 and 7: Faith as Refuge. Sermons 4 and 7, the short-est and perhaps the least allusive, are concerned neither with church polity nor with doctrinal controversy, subjects which in some form find their way into the other sermons. Both contain a message relying heavily upon Christian faith and extolling the virtue of patience, and both are concerned with privation or need: the type caused by grief (4) and the kind which compels men to pray (7).

Sermon 4, a funeral sermon for an anonymous "virtuous woman," is based on John 14:27. In the introduction, Hooker quotes an earlier verse from John, adding that he has "otherwhere already" spoken of it (3:644), a reference suggesting that a lost sermon was based upon this verse. Hooker analyzes the harmful nature of grief and explores situations in which grief is appropriate. He cites Christ's reproof of those who mistakenly grieved for him and develops the view that men should not grieve over the prosperity of the wicked. Yet one kind of grief may be acceptable, "The grief of compassion whereby we are touched with the feeling of other men's woes is of all other least dangerous" (3:646–47); on the other hand, grief over one's own sins represents great danger because it can lead to despair. Since grief is inevitable, the desirable course for the Christian is to cultivate patience, "that virtue which only hath power to stay our souls from being over-excessively troubled" (3:647).

Turning from his remedy for relief of the troubled heart, he moves to an analysis of fear in a tone as natural as a treatment of the subject might be in a treatise on ethics. As he so often does, he appeals to the concept of nature to establish that fear itself is grounded in nature and is thus no sin, at least not inherently. Some fear is necessary, as, for example, the fear of God, without which man becomes arrogant. Hooker turns this to advantage in a reference to Rome: "Is there any estate more fearful than that Babylonian strumpet's, that sitteth upon the tops of the seven hills glorying and vaunting . . . ?" (3:651). He concludes that to a Christian, Christ represents the refuge from fear.

The sermon demonstrates Hooker's quest for understanding rather than an effort to move the emotions. The occasion of a funeral is an ideal opportunity for an emotional appeal, but Hooker tells his audience what emotions are natural and explains how they should be understood.

The seventh sermon examines the efficacy of prayer, taking as its

text Matthew 7:7–8, "Ask and it shall be given you. . . ." It provides
a good illustration of Hooker's talent at organization, notably in the
divisio: "In which words we are first commanded to 'ask,' 'seek,' and
'knock:' secondly, promised grace answerable unto every of these
endeavours; . . . thirdly, this grace is particularly warranted, because
it is generally here averred, that no man asking, seeking, and knock-
ing, shall fail of that whereunto his serious desire tendeth" (3:701).
This brief sermon proceeds to treat in order the three parts outlined
with particular attention to the first.

In the introduction, which moves toward a statement of man's
dependence upon God, Hooker begins with an observation about
man's development: "As all the creatures of God, which attain their
highest perfection by process of time, are in their first beginning
raw; so man, in the end of his race the perfectest, is at his entrance
thereunto the weakest, and thereby longer enforced to continue a
subject for other men's compassions to work upon voluntarily, without any other persuader, besides their own secret inclination, moving
them to repay to the common stock of humanity such help, as they
know that themselves before must needs have borrowed; the state
and condition of all flesh being herein alike" (3:700). In this passage,
as in so many others, Hooker gives ample assurances that he is an
Aristotelian, and this intellectual cast, perhaps more than anything
else, separates him from his Puritan opponents.

Another characteristic of Hooker's thought that appears in sermon
7 is his desire to make everything clear and rational. His language
and style create an impression that matters normally considered mysterious and inexplicable are to him pellucid. When he comes to the
portion of the sermon that explains "promised grace answerable unto
every of these endeavours," he is faced with a logical impossibility:
"Are we in the case of them, who as yet do only ask and have not
received? . . . we shall find, but where?" (3:706). For this kind of
quandary, only faith can provide an answer: "we shall receive and
find in the end; it shall at length be opened unto you: however, or
by what means, leave it to God" (3:707). In plain prose, he assures
his audience that prayers are answered, but not always when and in
the way that they expect.

Sermons 5–6: False Prophecy and Schism.   Sermons 5 and 6
were published by Henry Jackson in 1614, under the title "Two
Sermons upon Part of St. Jude's Epistle." The sermons derive from
the same text, Jude 17–21, which warns about false prophets and

creators of sects and admonishes the believers to edify themselves. Sermon 5 is derived primarily from the first three verses, and sermon 6 from the last two. From internal evidence in sermon 5, the composition date appears to have been 1594, for Hooker says that for twenty-four years his countrymen have levied charges against the Church of England, an apparent reference to English Catholics abroad since the bull issued by Pope Pius V against Queen Elizabeth in 1570. If the conjectured composition date is correct, then the two sermons were delivered soon after the first four books of *Of the Laws of Ecclesiastical Polity* had been published. Since the sermons include telling points against Catholicism, or Babylon, as Hooker usually refers to it, they cast the author in the role of opponent of popery at a time when he was being accused by his Puritan opponents of leaning too far in the direction of Rome.

Early in sermon 5, Hooker is at pains to repudiate prophecy not derived from Scripture, "even they that are wisest amongst us living, compared with the prophets, seem no otherwise to talk of God, than as if the children which are carried in arms should speak of the greatest matters of state" (3:662), and those wise men acknowledge their own limitations, whereas true prophets of the Bible spoke with confidence and authority. But not all biblical prophecy is equally important, the most important being that which promises salvation to man through Christ. While men are to trust the prophecies of the Bible as supportive of faith, those prophets who came after the biblical era are false. Along with the Chaldeans, soothsayers, astrologers, and wizards, Hooker includes the false apostles of the Roman church: "No, we have no Lord but Jesus; no doctrine but the gospel; no teachers but his Apostles.... I do marvel, that any man bearing the name of a servant of the servants of Jesus Christ, will go about to draw us from our allegiance" (3:666).

Next he turns to scriptural prophecy concerning the "mockers," whom Hooker defines as those "men that shall use religion as a cloak, to put off and on, as the weather serveth..." (3:668), who throw off the restraints of religion in order to indulge their passions. The sermon proceeds to deal with heresy, schism, and apostasy as forces that separate Christians from the church and to denounce the papal policies that charge these against Englishmen. In a kind of digression, Hooker refutes the claim for papal authority based upon Matthew 16:18. The sermon concludes with an eloquent defense of Christianity in England against charges from Rome and from English exiles living in Europe. What began as a sermon against false prophets in the latter days concludes with a refutation of the charge that the English church itself is misleading its people.

Sermon 6 begins with a reference to the preceding sermon, giving its subject matter and making it clear that the work will be concerned with Jude 20–21, and admonishing believers to edify themselves and keep themselves "in the law of God." In this sermon, "edify," in the sense of build or construct, becomes a central metaphor through which Hooker exhorts his audience. It conveys a sense of immediacy between man's soul and God commonly found in Puritan prose, but not found so commonly in Hooker: "[God] hath written our names in the palm of his hand, in the signet upon his finger are we graven, in sentences not only of mercy, but of judgment also, we are remembered" (3:681). An analysis of God's judgments from the Bible serves to point out that God extends to man mercy along with judgment.

The sermon represents an exhortation to the faithful to strengthen their faith, with examples of the importance of faith drawn from the Old and New Testaments. But as to specific recommendations about how this is done, Hooker offers very little. He suggests the Lord's Supper, not as providing grace in itself but as giving man the occasion to reexamine often "these buildings of ours, in what case they stand" (3:686) and to repent if necessary. He scoffs at the idea that forgiveness can be obtained through indulgences, through the faith and works of others, or in any way other than through belief.

In a sermon which emphasizes Protestant individualism, Hooker turns at the end to admonish his hearers to reform themselves rather than the church. Some church polity is necessary and desirable, and that which works is not to be tampered with lightly. The metaphor of the individual building is extended to the church itself, and Hooker attempts to convey to his congregation the effect of ordered strength in the church, urging them to "keep yourselves in the law of God":

If the guide of a congregation...be diligent in his vocation, feeding the flock of God which dependeth upon him, caring for it...as a pattern unto the flock, wisely guiding them: if the people in their degree do yield themselves framable to the truth, not like rough stone or flint, refusing to be smoothed and squared for the building: if the magistrate

do carefully and diligently survey the whole order of the work, providing by statutes and laws, and bodily punishments, if need require, that
all things may be done according to the rule which cannot deceive...
there the words of this exhortation are truly and effectually heard. (3:696)

For the remainder of sermon 6, Hooker explores attitudes concerning
the defects of the church and its ministers, whom critics compare
unfavorably with those of earlier times. His metaphor of the building
serves well to bring about a resolution of the problem, one which
must have come as something of a surprise to the audience: "the
only way to repair all ruins, breaches, and offensive decays, in others,
is to begin reformation at yourselves" (3:699). Thus, Hooker's most
important concern is the individual soul and its faith.

    Sermons: Conclusion. To appreciate Hooker's sermons, one
must take into account his audience of baptized Christians of the late
sixteenth century. He does not feel compelled to consider questions
of salvation from the viewpoint of pre-Christian pagans or Jews, or
nonbelievers of his own time. Like the Protestant reformers he
emphasizes salvation through faith; the major themes of the first
three sermons—faith, salvation within churches which teach false
beliefs, and salvation as it relates to law—become important subjects in his later work. It may well be that his audience of law
students prompted his examination of justice and law in sermon 3,
which introduces ideas that are expanded in *Ecclesiastical Polity.*

    Hooker views law and societies governed through law as sup-
portive of salvation, man's final end: faith, law, and societies all
work in unison toward the same goal. This optimistic view and broad
understanding of law will lead him later to argue that willful disobedience to lawful authority, if persisted in, is sinful and jeopardizes
salvation.

    The sermons also reflect Hooker's effort to find the middle ground
between the Puritans and the Catholic church. Since the most familiar
passages in Hooker assail Puritans, he is often envisioned as an opponent of Puritanism. The sermons include numerous attacks on Catholic
theology and policy, a theme of special prominence in his later works,
and suggest the need for a more balanced view. Above all, the sermons reflect Hooker's Aristotelianism—his effort to find a mean, his
analytical cast, his quest for moderation, his concern with ends, and
his essentially unified view.

Replies to Attacks

The *Answer to Travers.*   The writings of Hooker reveal a
strong inclination to differentiate between matters of church polity and
matters of salvation; he usually draws a sharper distinction between
the two than do his adversaries. In general, his minor works deal
with questions involving salvation and theological issues, while the
major work deals with church polity. But in the *Answer to Travers*,
this second issue receives significant attention.

*Mr. Hooker's Answer to the Supplication That Mr. Travers Made
to the Council* was written in 1586, though not printed until 1612,
when Henry Jackson published his edition. The *Answer* is addressed
to the archbishop of Canterbury, the ranking church official on the
Privy Council. Travers had addressed his *Supplication* to the Privy
Council itself, thus appealing over the archbishop. Hooker justifies
his reply on the grounds that Travers had circulated numerous copies
of his appeal and that Travers's charges against him might be
credited if he remained silent on the matter.

Travers's *Supplication*, like Hooker's reply, is for the most part
moderate and reasonable in tone. Before coming to his disagreement with Hooker, he pleads against the severity of his being silenced,
as well as the manner of it, and attempts to explain his ordination
abroad. He takes an occasional opportunity to suggest that Puritans
like him have been treated more severely than Catholics, but overall
his tone suggests sincerity and sobriety.

In the two thirds of the pamphlet devoted to his disagreement
with Hooker, Travers charges Hooker with "unsound doctrine" concerning predestination, the validity of private reason, and the Catholic
church. After quoting at some length from Hooker's sermon 2, he
remarks: "I think the like to this . . . hath not been heard in public
places within this land since Queen Mary's days" (3:567). Travers
thus took the occasion to embarrass Hooker for his liberal position
regarding Catholics at a time when the nation was strongly anti-
Catholic. Though his pamphlet did not succeed either in discrediting
Hooker or in gaining a remission of the archbishop's order, it did
prompt Hooker to reply.

In his *Answer*, Hooker naturally devotes attention to the portion
of Travers's pamphlet that concerned himself, largely ignoring Travers's complaints about the proceeding of the archbishop. The *Answer*
deals with specific charges, the first being that Hooker is of a surly

and unpeaceable disposition. He gives a detailed account of the disagreements over procedure in church service, including Travers's objections to every particular. The basis for Travers's charge appears to have been Hooker's rejection of his innovations at the Temple church.

As for doctrine, Travers had complained that many of Hooker's sermons "tasted of some sour leaven or other" and had challenged Hooker's belief regarding predestination (3:576). From Hooker's sermons and his later treatise it is abundantly clear that he was not temperamentally suited to this grim doctrine. He would have been regarded by Puritans as a Pelagian, or, in a later time, an Arminian, a position then accepted by the majority of prelates and even by some Puritans, Milton included. But the Anglican theology of Hooker's day was influenced by Calvin, and he seems unwilling to probe deeply into the theological questions. His main defense is that when he preached the sermon in question, Bishop Aylmer was present and had found no objectionable doctrine. A second objection was to Hooker's statement that sensory perception provides greater assurance to man than he acquires through his faith, a charge which he analyzes rationally and refutes.

Concerning Hooker's preaching about Rome, Travers had attributed to Hooker the viewpoint that the Church of England agreed with Rome on major issues and disagreed only on minor points. Hooker's reply includes material which suggests that Travers had misunderstood his sermon, the effect being that Travers's objection seems zealous and captious.

In his quarrel with Hooker, Travers's chief offense, which he had attempted to gloss over and explain away, concerned his action—preaching publicly against Hooker without first conferring with him. This act was prohibited by canon law, and Hooker will not let Travers forget it. As he often does, he resorts to a rhetorical question to clarify an important or difficult point of controversy: "Is this the rule of Christ, If thy brother offend openly in his speech, control it first with contrary speech openly, and confer with him afterwards upon it, when convenient opportunity serveth?" (3:590).

Among other minor objections, Travers had charged that Hooker taught against the testimony of "all good writers" (3:592) and had then brought Hooker a passage from Peter Martyr's commonplace book that had no ascertainable bearing on the issue at hand. In a brief account of his view concerning predestination, Hooker argues that the foreknowledge of God does not cause evil among men, that God permits evil rather than causes it, and that election is conditional, "the will of God in this thing is not absolute but conditional, to save his elect believing, fearing, and obediently serving him..." (3:592–93). At the end of the pamphlet Hooker returns to the charge that Travers had gone beyond acceptable action in attacking him from the pulpit and expresses the desire for controversy in the church to end: "I take no joy in striving, I have not been nuzzled or trained up in it" (3:596).

The Answer to *A Christian Letter.*   Probably the final work of Hooker's pen, except for his will, is a rough draft of an answer to an attack on the fifth book of *Ecclesiastical Polity* by an anonymous Puritan author, *A Christian Letter of Certain English Protestants* (1599). In his copy of the book, Hooker wrote pointed and often indignant answers to specific charges in the *Christian Letter* and began an answer which he apparently intended for eventual publication. The "Fragments of an Answer to the Letter of certain English Protestants" remained in manuscript until its discovery by Archdeacon Cotton and subsequent publication by Keble in 1836. Highly theological, the work concerns free will, grace, the sacraments, and predestination, the longest portion being devoted to predestination. Near the end of his life Hooker undertakes serious exploration of a theological belief that had been treated briefly in his St. Paul's Cross sermon, in sermon 2, and in the *Answer to Travers.*

It is a work of significance because Hooker attempts a further clarification of his views on important theological issues. In *Ecclesiastical Polity*, theology can be and often is secondary to an explanation and defense of external order. Hooker can take the position that he and his opponents have no serious disagreements about theology, only about matters of church polity. Not only were the Puritans unwilling to separate polity and belief, but from the beginning they attempted to find error in Hooker's view of predestination, the incarnation, the Trinity, and other theological questions. For the most part, Hooker sought to avoid theological controversies, though his fifth book does include extensive discussions of the incarnation, the sacraments, and grace.

Regarding freedom of the will, he upholds the power in man, although he acknowledges that the will is assisted by grace. God's powers and providence do not change man's voluntary nature, "Prescience, predestination, and grace, impose not that necessity, by force whereof man in doing good hath all freedom of choice taken from him" (2:538). Hooker reviews in this section the Pelagian heresy and its resolution, and without naming Calvin seems to deny the doctrine of Irresistibility of Grace: "*Pelagius* urged labour for the attainment of eternal life without necessity of God's grace: if we teach grace without necessity of man's labour, we use one error as a nail to drive out another" (2:549).

When he turns to the question regarding the sacraments and grace, he explains the characteristics of sacraments and restates the Anglican position that there are only two: Baptism and the Lord's Supper. After initial justification, works are necessary: "Now between the grace of this first justification, and the glory of the world to come, whereof we are not capable, unless the rest of our lives be qualified with the righteousness of a second justification consisting in good works, therefore as St. *Paul* doth dispute for faith without works to the first, so St. James to the second justification is urgent for works with faith" (2:553). Sacraments are neither mere signs designed for instruction nor direct conveyers of grace but signs as tokens of God's promised grace, which affects man internally.

When he answers the article regarding predestination, Hooker has his greatest difficulty. In his time, theologians in the Church of England were usually Calvinistic, and those whom Hooker respected, including Whitgift, would have upheld belief in predestination. The Lambeth Articles, formulated under Whitgift in 1595 though never officially approved, represented a shift toward Calvin among leading churchmen. Yet predestination was a doctrine Hooker avoided and naturally felt uncomfortable with. He had stressed the freedom of man's will, the necessity of faith, and a belief that God's general will was good, that Christ had died for all men, that grace is sufficient—all of which limit predestination.

To examine the question Hooker distinguishes between necessary and contingent causes. It is necessary for a man to be rational but contingent for a man to be learned, a condition produced by a variety of secondary causes. Belief in divine providence is the midpoint between belief in unalterable destiny and belief in pure chance. God's foreknowledge or prescience does not cause events to occur, as numerous scriptural references demonstrate. Not only does God foresee events which He does not cause, as Christ foresaw the betrayal of Judas, but He foresees events that do not actually occur, as when God enabled David to save himself by warning him that the Lords of Kerlah would deliver him over to Baal. God's purpose in creating and governing the world is good, and therefore a supralapsarian position, the extreme Calvinistic position that God willed the fall of Adam, is untenable (2:566).

On the contrary, God destined created beings to happiness. Man as represented in Adam sinned through his own choice, and the views which attributed man's original sin to God are heretical. After sin awakened God's wrath and brought about the need for justice, some men were required to suffer for their sins, the sentence of justice being proportionable to sin. Yet God provides both eternal life and grace to repent, and God's general inclination for man's good continues despite sins: "he inclineth still ... that all men may enjoy the full perfection of that happiness, which is their end ..." and, "He longeth for nothing more than that all men might be saved" (2:573).

Yet not all are saved, for God has a secondary or consequent will, whereby those suffer punishment who through their fault deserve to suffer. Hooker examines at length the controversy between Augustine and his followers and the Pelagians, with a detailed account of the interpretation of Augustine's teaching by the Synod at Arles (ca. 475).

The outward grace by which God through the church brings men to faith and repentance has not been universally found. Inward grace through which men come to salvation is sometimes ineffective because men burden their own hearts and are justly condemned. "Though grace therefore be lost by desert, yet [it] is not by desert given" (2:595).

In a brief fragment concerning Travers's objections to Hooker's sermon of 28 March 1585, included by John Strype in his revision of Walton's *Life of Hooker*, Travers lists fifteen points, most concerned with Catholicism, but three concerned with predestination. Hooker taught, he says, the following:

> Predestination is not the absolute will of God, but conditional.
> The doings of the wicked are not of the will of God positive, but only permissive.
> The reprobates are not rejected, but for the evil works which God did foresee they would commit. (1:60)

Significantly, Hooker's answer to these points does not survive, only to major ones concerned with the church of Rome and the archbishop's judgment on these. In this final section of his reply to *A Christian Letter*, he lists eight points and a qualification concerning predestination. Based upon the nine Lambeth Articles, his more liberal points support predestination more strongly than he had done before, but do not alter the opinion that Travers attributes to him. His fourth point supports two and three above, "That it cannot be but their sins must condemn them, to whom the purpose of his saving mercy doth not extend" (2:596). The others express general support for the view that certain men, not all, are predestined to salvation, that man's virtue or good does not cause the choice, that the number is known to God, that they are given continuance of grace, that inward grace to salvation without which no man can come to Christ is not given to all men, and that it is not within the individual's power to be saved.[4] But he adds, as if to confirm his essential point from the sermon, "Howbeit, God is no favourer of sloth; and therefore there can be no such absolute decree, touching man's salvation as on our part includeth no necessity of care and travail . . ." (2:596–97)—that is, predestination is conditional, and with this qualification the "Fragments of an Answer" ends.

When Hooker found it necessary to confront belief in predestination, he had to face other grim realities: that the Jews were God's chosen people, and the rest were hardened; that since the time of Christ, most men had been non-Christians. Some selective process was obviously at work, however unpleasant to face. He found himself having to accept a modified form of a doctrine accepted by his church, his mentors and friends, but one inimical to his nature. It deflected his mind from that vision of unity within a harmonious structure and order, toward that other reality of suffering and discord.

It is not certain that the position outlined in "Fragments of an Answer" represents Hooker's final view of the matter, for the work is incomplete. In 1603, William Covel, a young clergyman, published a reply to *A Christian Letter* entitled *A Just and Temperate Defense of the Five Books of Ecclesiastical Policie*. It responds to all of the twenty-one points raised in the attack on Hooker and is dedicated to Archbishop Whitgift. Covel's work reveals no indication that he had access to Hooker's unpublished writings.

Chapter Three
Ecclesiastical Polity, Books 1-4 : First Principles

Hooker's *Of the Laws of Ecclesiastical Polity* has a long and complicated publishing history. Of the eight books, only five appeared in print during the author's lifetime; the first four books were published in 1593, and book 5, longer than those four together, appeared in 1597. It seems likely that publication of books 1–4 was arranged to coincide with the debate in Parliament of an anticonventicle bill supported by Edwin Sandys, Hooker's former pupil, who bore the expense of publication.[1]

Books 1–4 represent the most basic and general positions of Hooker's treatise. The discussion of law in book 1 forms the groundwork for his justification of the church polity, and book 4 defends the established church against the broad Puritan charge that it retains too many Catholic rites and ceremonies. Books 2 and 3 refute Puritan positions on the authority of Scripture and Scripture as the sole basis of church polity. These two books thus constitute an attack on Puritan views, whereas books 1 and 4 provide positive support for the *status quo.*

Preface

The first four books, the most familiar portion of *Ecclesiastical Polity*, were accompanied by a preface of nine chapters, which Hooker addressed to those who sought further reform of the Church of England. It accomplishes a great deal—introducing the reader to the basic positions that *Ecclesiastical Polity* will defend and attempting to account for and discredit the Puritan movement. In his famous statement justifying his work, Hooker writes, "that posteritie may know we have not loosely through silence permitted things to passe away as in a dreame, there shall be for mens information extant thus much concerning the present state of the Church of God established amongst us...."[2]

Introduction to the Treatise. Hooker's primary purpose is to defend the established church against its Puritan opponents, and he expects no better treatment at their hands for his work than they accorded others who had made the same effort. After a brief examination of the Puritan position, Hooker concludes as his "finall resolute persuasion": (1) "the present forme of Churchgovernment... is such, as no lawe of God, nor reason of man hath hitherto bene alleaged of force sufficient to prove they do ill, who to the uttermost of their power withstand the alteration thereof," and (2) "The other... is only by error and misconceipt named the ordinance of Jesus Christ" (Pref., 1.2). In his preface, Hooker goes a long way toward developing the second position against the Puritans, and it therefore reads more like a religious polemic or tract, whereas the work in its entirety reads like a treatise of church government.

In his seventh chapter, Hooker provides an outline of the eight books, an outline repeated in a table of contents that follows the preface, even though only four of the eight books are being published. The work divides into two parts of four books each, the first group consisting of those dealing with generalities. Four additional books "are bestowed about the specialities of that cause which lyeth in controversie" (Pref., 7.6); that is, they concern more specific points of controversy. It should be noted that Hooker speaks here of "the whole intier bodie" (Pref., 7.7) of his work as a coherent whole, as if it were complete or nearly complete. Elsewhere in the preface he writes of what "as in the last booke of this treatise we have shewed at large" (Pref., 8.2), an assertion which led John Keble to conclude that *Ecclesiastical Polity* had been completed by the time the first books appeared.[3]

Address to the Puritans. A second major purpose of the preface is to refute or challenge the various Puritan positions, and in doing so Hooker traces the origins of the Presbyterian discipline, explains its appeal and dangers, and considers the Puritans' call for a conference on church polity. In the long second chapter, he gives an account of Calvin's success in Geneva, not without praise of Calvin as a theologian. Significantly, he views Geneva as too egalitarian in its civil government to be representative of other cities and states. In clarifying conditions out of which Calvinism grew, he makes it apparent that England is not suited for the Presbyterian church polity that established itself in Geneva. Hooker believes that Calvin began his movement in a kind of power vacuum where church polity was concerned, with only opposition to Catholicism generally agreed upon in the city. Even in such a vacuum, Calvin encountered difficulties and reverses and had to make compromises. A major one had to do with putting laymen on the ecclesiastical court, which Hooker stresses is not biblical—a point that would seem to damage that religious polity which justifies all its parts as founded on the Bible.

In accounting for the appeal of Calvinist discipline, Hooker suggests that it involves unlearned laity in matters of church polity, a matter beyond their capacities. In effect, he charges that the Puritans are astute propagandists, carrying the day with unlearned people through oversimplification, false dilemmas, and emotional appeals. As an example of the extreme he names the Family of Love for their mystical and symbolic interpretation of Scripture and its application to doctrine and society. A further stage in the Puritan appeal is to persuade the credulous that anyone can discover the obscure points of Scripture through "the speciall illumination of the holy Ghost" (Pref., 3.10).

On this position Hooker makes a point central to his entire work: "There are but two waies whereby the spirit leadeth men into all truth: the one extraordinarie, the other common; the one belonging but unto some few, the other extending it selfe unto all that are of God; the one that which we call by a speciall divine excellency *Revelation*, the other *Reason*" (Pref., 3.10). He insists that the new order must stand the test of reason, in part because he is confident that it will not. For the Puritans, having convinced themselves that they are led by the Holy Spirit, separate themselves into "*The* brethren, *The* godlie" and willingly communicate only with each other. Thus he traces the appeals—the psychological factors—which attract and hold simple people to the Puritan discipline: the custom of blaming and attacking faults in governors, attributing the faults to church polity, holding up the Puritan discipline as a panacea, professing that Scripture supports the new discipline in all points, assuming illumination through the Holy Spirit, and assuming that this illumination is in itself assurance of the person's nearness to God.

Having accounted for the appeal and successes of the new discipline among the unlearned, Hooker tries to account for its hold upon ministers, scholars, and writers generally. The idea of restoring an apostolic model exerts a strong appeal, despite its limitations: weak scriptural authority, absence of precedent, and the long approval through history of an episcopal order. The theologians who have defended the new order have caused numerous others to accept it, even though, Hooker says, they disagree among themselves.

Hooker next turns to the Puritans' call for a public debate on church polity, appeals which took different forms. Some wanted a conference with public debaters; others, a debate in writing with the results to be published afterward. He sees no problem in debates being carried on at universities but opposes official church participation. Nothing illustrates Hooker's difference with the Puritans better than this section of his preface. He regards their position as revolutionary, his own as evolutionary. The Puritans are really asking that laws be suspended until they can be persuaded by public debate to obey them. Hooker's vision of law precludes this kind of license: "A lawe is the deed of the whole bodie politike, whereof if ye judge your selves to be any part, then is the law even your deed also" (Pref., 5.2). It follows that the law is to be obeyed until it has been repealed.

He proposes a carefully controlled conference, in which the Puritans must be willing to accept the role of plaintiff or opponent and agree to recognize some final authority that would resolve all questions. He proposes three additional rules for the conference: that general questions be dealt with first, that the Puritans acknowledge beforehand one chief spokesman to present their views, and that one published account of the conference be circulated. This set of restrictions, which seemed reasonable enough to Hooker, the Puritans could not have accepted, for the rules would have meant a denial of private interpretation of matters of church polity.

Like Whitgift, Hooker recognized at the time that the Puritans' quarrels with particulars of church worship were only tactical, concealing a larger purpose of overturning the entire ecclesiastical structure. He makes a plea, nonetheless, for the Puritans to accept the kind of authority that could put an end to contention, citing the Council of Jerusalem (Acts 15) as a biblical precedent for resolution of disputes and stressing that private individuals are more likely to err than collective bodies of thoughtful and informed leaders. Though he has little hope that the Puritans will accept the rule of any existing authority without a conference, he holds out hope that a general council would be respected. Meanwhile, Puritans are bound to obey laws that are established: "As for the orders which are established, sith equitie and reason, the law of nature, God and man, do all favour

that which is in being, till orderlie judgement of decision be given
against it; it is but justice to exact of you, and perversnes in you it
should be to denie thereunto your willing obedience" (Pref., 6.5).

In his eighth chapter Hooker turns to the dangers of separation,
which to him means anarchy, the extremes of Henry Barrowe, for
example, as derived from Puritan principles. Here again he sees
church and state as all of a piece and observes that innovation in
church polity will affect all the orders of society, including the universities, corporations, and law. But the greatest danger from the
Puritans is what C. S. Lewis called their Barthian reductiveness[4] in
holding "that your discipline being ... the absolute commaundement
of almighty God, it must be received although the world by receiving
it should be cleane turned upside downe ..." (Pref., 8.5).

As an example of the extremes to which Puritan principles can lead,
Hooker gives a lengthy account of the Anabaptists of Meunster, based
primarily upon the work of Guy de Brès (1565). It is significant that
in his text Hooker does not name the Anabaptist leaders, nor does he
use the words "Anabaptist" and "Meunster." For he perceives the
movement, not as derived from the insanity or fanaticism of leaders,
not as wild and reckless enthusiasm, but as the logical result of principles and assumptions followed to their conclusion without restric-
tion or restraint. Although the Anabaptist movement was remote
from Hooker in time and place, he finds in it similarities to the
Puritans of his own time, particularly in the divisions and the excesses
that were becoming all too apparent. The Anabaptists, like the Puritans,
accepted no authority but that of Scripture, and Scripture as they
read it seemed to sanction the overthrow of all existing institutions.
In England, the activities of Robert Browne, Henry Barrowe, John
Penry, and others during the 1580s and 1590s seemed to indicate a
drift in the direction of anarchy, so much so that even Cartwright
had found it necessary to renounce the extreme separatists.

Hooker demonstrates that he understands the psychology of revolutionary movements by drawing a comparison between the Anabaptists and the Puritans:

Now what soever they did in such sort collect out of Scripture when they
came to justifie or perswade it unto others, all was the heavenly fathers
appointment, his commaundement, his will and charge.... [W]hen the
minds of men are once erroniously perswaded that it is the will of God
to have those things done which they phancie, their opinions are as

thornes in their sides never suffering them to take rest till they have
brought their speculations into practise.... (Pref., 8.12)

Defiance by the Puritans of authority and law, both civil and religious,
justifies a fear that danger similar to that of the Anabaptists exists.
The example of the Anabaptists is used, not to condemn the Puritan
movement wholesale, but to urge the moderate Puritans to consider
where their defiance of authority might lead. Hooker seems confident
that the extremes of the Anabaptists hold as much fear for most
Puritans as for him.

The conclusion of this preface is a plea for harmony in the church
and reconciliation with the Puritans. Hooker asks the Puritans to
reexamine their position systematically, argument by argument, seemingly confident that once they have done so they will abandon it.
In so doing, he is calling for a rational approach to the issues which
divide them, citing as a precedent St. Augustine's retraction of earlier
errors.

Book 1: Concerning Laws

Book 1, "Concerning Lawes, and their severall kindes in generall,"
represents the most familiar portion of Hooker's work, the source of
most quotations from Hooker. For here he lays down his basic principles, distinctions, and definitions—the groundwork for a logical defense of church polity. Beginning with law he transcends the Puritan
reliance upon Scripture, a necessity if he is to succeed in refuting
that position. His exposure to law at the Temple no doubt stood him
in good stead, for he examines not only the nature and types of laws,
but also goes into the factors that account for their origins. Long
before the book ends he has made the Puritans' scripturalism look
altogether too narrow and, in large measure, untenable. To the
modern reader, the book forms the most valuable introduction to the
breadth of Hooker's intellectual vision and to his unified system of
values and assumptions.

The well-known opening deals with men's usual assumptions about
existing institutions: "He that goeth about to perswade a multitude,
that they are not so well governed as they ought to be, shall never
want attentive and favourable hearers; because they know the mani-
fold defects whereunto every kind of regiment is subject, but the
secret lets and difficulties, which in publike proceedings are innu-

merable and inevitable, they have not ordinarily the judgement to consider" (1.1.1). Faced with this reality, defenders of the established order are at a disadvantage because they will be suspected as time-servers.

Still another disadvantage is the inherent complexity of the subject. Writing of order in metaphors later used by Dryden and Burke, the architectural metaphor and the metaphor of the tree, Hooker describes the organic nature of the church and state:

The statelinesse of houses, the goodlines of trees, when we behold them delighteth the eye; but that foundation which beareth up the one, that root which ministreth unto the other nourishment and life, is in the bosome of the earth concealed: and if there be at any time occasion to search into it, such labour is then more necessary then pleasant both to them which undertake it, and for the lookers on. In like maner the use and benefite of good lawes, all that live under them may enjoy with delight and comfort, albeit the groundes and first originall causes from whence they have sprong be unknowne, as to the greatest part of men they are. (1.1.2)

Not only is there a kind of organic unity in the church; Hooker attempts to reflect that unity in his work, as he explains: "I have endevoured throughout the bodie of this whole discourse, that every former part might give strength unto all that followe, and every later bring some light unto all before" (1.1.2).

Law Defined.   To the reader accustomed to thinking of a law as a written rule, Hooker's definition of the term represents a surprising expansion. He begins much in the manner of Aristotle and Aquinas, dealing with though not analyzing the various kinds of *causes*. Then he moves quickly to his first definition of *law*:

All things that are have some operation not violent or casuall. Neither doth any thing ever begin to exercise the same without some foreconceaved ende for which it worketh. And the ende which it worketh for is not obteined, unlesse the worke be also fit to obteine it by. For unto every ende every operation will not serve. That which doth assigne unto each thing the kinde, that which doth moderate the force and power, that which doth appoint the forme and measure of working, the same we tearme a *Lawe*. (1.2.1)

Elsewhere he defines law, consistently to be sure, but more simply, "any kind of rule or canon whereby actions are framed" (1.3.1) or "a directive rule unto goodnes of operation" (1.8.4). He recognizes that his definitions imply an even broader meaning than he attributes to law, and, of course, it is unnecessary that laws be written to have binding force.

Laws Eternal. Even God works in eternal decrees through some principle, Hooker writes, though the divine law remains beyond man's understanding. He quotes pagan philosophers who saw the First Cause as acting in accordance with Reason "that is to say, constant *order* and *law* is kept..." (1.2.3). As to the working of God, the following passage illustrates how Hooker sees "law," "reason," "will," "causation," and "teleology" all connected: "God worketh nothing without cause. All those things which are done by him, have some ende for which they are done: and the ende for which they are done, it a reason of his will to do them" (1.2.3). Even though some of God's reasons and ends are hidden, so central are reason and law from Hooker's standpoint that they become *a priori* principles, matters of faith: "The particular drift of everie acte proceeding externally from God, we are not able to discerne, and therefore cannot alwaies give the proper and certaine reason of his works. Howbeit undoubtedly a proper and certaine reason there is of every finite worke of God, in as much as there is a law imposed upon it..." (1.2.4). The rational nature of God is reflected in his created order, and like Einstein, Hooker would not have believed that the Almighty casts dice.

The law of God's own being and purposes Hooker terms the "first law eternal." A second law eternal governs the will, actions, development, and alteration of all created beings: "that which with himselfe he hath set downe as expedient to be kept by all his creatures, according to the severall condition wherwith he hath indued them" (1.3.1). All other categories or classifications of law are derived from this second law, including the law of nature, the law of angels, the law of reason, the scriptural law, and *human law* "that which out of the law either of reason or of God, men probablie gathering to be expedient, they make it a law" (1.3.1). Human law is of three types, depending upon what governs: commonweal, politic societies, and nations.

Laws of Nature and Angels. Hooker treats in turn the kinds of law designated by the second law eternal, and of these the first is natural law, that which applies to involuntary agents. The existence of such a law is confirmed by the Mosaic account of the creation:

"His commanding those things to be which are, and to be in such sort as they are, to keep that tenure and course which they do, importeth the establishment of natures law" (1.3.2). The existence of a natural law derived from God implies an originally perfect order in nature; Hooker attributes nature's manifest imperfection to the Fall. Yet he sees the overall order as admirable, fulfilling God's purpose, and directed by Providence. In a very short concluding paragraph he suggests that natural agents also have a social law whereby the action of an individual agent may defy its own nature to serve a larger good, his only example being "that which is heavie mounting sometime upwardes of it owne accord, and forsaking the centre of the earth, which to it selfe is most naturall, . . . to releive the present distresse of nature in common" (1.3.5). In a unified and hierarchical world view, this example might well become an argument by analogy for rational, voluntary man to subordinate his own private will and interest to those of the established church and state.

In his treatment of the law of angels, it is this social sense or compact that interests Hooker most. The actions and orders of angels involve adoration, love, and imitation of God through their deeds, and such is their order that Christ in his prayer used it as the appropriate model for men on earth. The angels more than nature "are lincked into a kinde of corporation amongst themselves, and of societie or fellowship with men" (1.4.2). Individually, they love and praise God, as groups or "as an *Army*, one in order and degree above another" (1.4.2). They associate with each other and God, and they further are bound to do ministerial employment among men, in imitation of God's perfect working.

Law of Reason or of Human Nature. Turning to law as it affects man and moves him toward perfection, Hooker reasserts his basic acceptance of teleology: "God alone excepted . . . all other things besides are somewhat in possibilitie, which as yet they are not in act. And for this cause there is in all things an appetite or desire, whereby they inclyne to something which they may be: and when they are it, they shall be perfecter then nowe they are" (1.5.1). How teleology may easily be adapted to Christianity is illustrated by Hooker's development of this idea: "all things in the worlde are saide in some sort to seeke the highest, and to covet more or lesse the participation of God himselfe" (1.5.2). Man seeks the perfection of God through such things as his desire for immortality, for offspring, for constancy, for excellence, for wisdom and virtue; and, appropriately, he seeks his development through knowledge: "The soule of man being therefore at the first as a booke, wherein nothing is, and yet all thinges may be imprinted; we are to search by what steppes and degrees it ryseth unto perfection of knowledge" (1.6.1).

Though he has no complex epistemology such as that of Hobbes, he believes that man begins to acquire knowledge through sensation, then through natural reason learns to generalize and weigh ideas, and through education and instruction to distinguish good from evil. Turning to account for moral action and precepts, Hooker assumes that man has an inherent need to act, an impulse to action, derived from God. Also derived from God is man's capacity of acting through choice: "that [which] we doe unto any such ende, the same we choose and preferre before the leaving of it undone" (1.7.2). All human action, then, springs from knowledge and from will, which is almost synonymous with choice.

He further explores the matter of will and choice when he considers the promptings of "appetite," which to Hooker includes more than desire for sensible good—"Affections, as joy, and griefe, and feare, and anger ... being as it were the sundry fashions and formes of appetite ..." (1.7.3). To explain the predominance of "will," he resorts to a legal metaphor, "appetite is the wills sollicitor, and the will is appetites controller ..." (1.7.3). He would not consider appetite a just reason for professing that some acts are involuntary and therefore not the responsibility of the actor: "The truth is, that such actions in men having attained to the use of reason are voluntary" (1.7.3). Since reason is the higher power, when the will does not dissent, it assents. Whatever the soundness of the philosophical position, it is unassailable as a legal position.

The will, he holds, does not direct man toward good, however desirable, if the goal is impossible. On this point he seems not far from Hume's emphasis on probability as the great guide in life. On the other hand, left entirely free to choose, the will makes many wrong choices, aberrancies attributable to many causes, the chief being man's fallen state. What seems clear and easy enough in principle becomes confused and difficult in practice:

In doing evill, we prefer a lesse good before a greater, the greatnes whereof is by reason investigable, and may be known. The search of knowledg is a thing painful and the painfulnes of knowledge is that which maketh the will so hardly inclinable thereunto. The root hereof

divine malediction whereby the instruments being weakned wherewithall
the soule (especially in reasoning) doth worke, it preferreth rest in ig-
norance before wearisome labour to knowe. (1.7.7)

Only after explaining their basis in human psychology can he
turn to an account of how man's reason discovers human laws. Man
by nature inclines toward actions, reason instructs him, and the will
makes the choice of direction and action—the aim of man's action
being goodness. Goodness is understood through either of two related
courses: understanding its causes or perceiving "signes and tokens"
annexed unto goodness. Of the second type, the surest sign is the
universal agreement of mankind: "The generall and perpetuall voyce
of men is as the sentence of God him selfe. For that which all men
have at all times learned, nature her selfe must needes have taught;
and God being the author of nature, her voyce is but his instrument"
(1.8.3). This example bears a relationship to the first method, for
universal assent implies causes, a basis in the first and superior method
of discerning goodness through reason: "The rule of voluntary agents
on earth is the sentence that reason giveth concerning the goodnes of
those things which they are to do" (1.8.4). Hooker regards the main
principles of reason as apparent and lists six axioms or principles to
be regarded as *a priori.* Even though they have the universal assent
of mankind, they were "at the first found out by discourse, and drawne
from out of the very bowels of heaven and earth" (1.8.5).

Reason provides man with three types of counsel—mandatory, per-
missive, or admonitory, "opening what is the most convenient for us
to doe" (1.8.8). But the law of reason, the law of human nature,
concerns what is mandatory: "that which men by discourse of naturall
reason have rightly found out themselves to be all for ever bound
unto in their actions" (1.8.8). To Hooker this law includes belief in
God, in immortality, and in the existence of the soul, as well as a
number of ethical principles, though nothing that requires revelation
for support. Laws of human nature lie within the power of the
common man to discover through discourse and reason. Hooker agrees
with Augustine in repudiating the notion that morals or ethics vary
merely according to culture, for the law of reason includes universally
accepted principles: "out of those principles, which are in themselves
evident, the greatest morall duties we owe towards God or man, may
without any great difficultie be concluded" (1.8.10), including the
love of God and man affirmed in the New Testament. Cultures depart

from the law of human nature (an example being idolatry), not because the law is inaccessible to their reason, but because they do not make an effort to discover it; since man may regress as well as progress, failure to make the effort causes him to be further blinded.

Laws of Commonweal, Politic Societies, and Nations. The law of reason instructs man in the need for some form of social order, though not in a specific type of order. A social order is founded through the law of commonweal and directed through the laws of politic societies, derived from "probable collections what is convenient for men ..." (1.8.11). Tracing the reasons for the beginnings of societies, Hooker follows the reasoning of the ancients, first calling attention to the utilitarian motive: "But for as much as we are not by our selves sufficient to furnish ourselves with competent store of things needfull for such a life as our nature doth desire, a life fit for the dignitie of man: therefore to supply those defects and imperfections, which are in us living, single, and solelie by our selves, we are naturally induced to seeke communion and fellowship with others" (1.10.1). Societies are supported by two foundations—"a naturall inclination, wherby all men desire sociable life and fellowship" and "an order expresly or secretly agreed upon, touching the manner of their union in living together" (1.10.1). The agreed upon order is designated "Law of a Commonweal," and, significantly, the concept of an original agreement makes the order similar to a social contract. Hooker assumes that at a definite time men gathered to establish the social contract, and, following Aristotle, that they took as the basic model the family. A patriarchal family order suggests a monarchy as the appropriate type of government for society, but Hooker acknowledges that other forms of government are legitimate.

Laws politic in society are first formulated to designate right or wrong not readily apparent to the judgments of most men. Further, rewards and punishments are annexed to laws to prevent every man from following his own private interest exclusively. The measure of reward or punishment "belongeth unto them by whome lawes are made" (1.10.6). Laws collectively created to uphold a social order Hooker designates "positive laws." They differ markedly from natural law in that they do not have universal binding force. Hooker admires the majesty and dignity of law, yet he hedges concerning the authority for establishing laws. Just as all types of law derive from divine laws, all authority derives ultimately from God:

That which wee spake before concerning the power of government must
here be applyed unto the power of making lawes whereby to governe,
which power God hath over all, and by the naturall lawe whereunto hee
hath made all subject, the lawfull power of making lawes to commande
whole politique societies of men belongeth so properly unto the same
intire societies, that for any Prince or potentate of what kinde soever
upon earth to excercise the same of him selfe and not either by expresse
commission immediatly and personally receyved from God, or els by
authoritie derived at the first from their consent upon whose persons they
impose lawes, it is no better then meere tyrannye. (1.10.8)

This passage seems to imply, at least indirectly, consent of the governed and to suggest that in English society Parliament is the normal
body for making laws, just as councils are in churches. Establishment
of a law does not require everyone's consent: "As in parliaments,
councels, and the like assemblies, although we be not personallie our
selves present, notwithstanding our assent is by reason of others
agents there in our behalfe" (1.10.8), an arrangement which is
binding. Furthermore, the authority of a positive law, once established,
is not limited by time "because corporations are immortall: we were
then alive in our predecessors, and they in their successors do live
still" (1.10.8).

Positive laws reveal great variety, depending upon the nature and
condition of the society they regulate. Some reaffirm laws of nature
and are thus human laws "mixedly"; others are "meerly" human laws,
based upon that "which reason doth but probablie teach to be fit and
convenient" (1.10.10), an example being laws governing inheritance.
Both civil and ecclesiastical societies make mixed and merely human
laws.

A third type of man-made law exists in laws of nations, designed
to regulate affairs among the world's nations. Among Christian
churches, as among nations, general councils may serve as a means
of promoting beneficial laws. Though he acknowledges that the use
of councils has fallen into disfavor during his own time, Hooker
strongly supports the idea of counciliar governance: "I nothing doubt
but that Christian men should much better frame them selves to
those heavenly preceptes, which our Lorde and Saviour with so great
instancie gave as concerning peace and unitie, if we did all concurre
in desire to have the use of auncient councels againe renued..."
(1.10.15).

Scriptural Law. Before discussing scriptural law, Hooker explains why it is necessary. Perfect happiness in human life is not possible, because man is incapable of attaining his desire for infinite good (i.e., God). No other creature can enjoy contemplating what is infinite, since the perfection of all creatures but man is limited to what can be achieved during their natural lives. Man aspires to more, and in his aspiration lies his great dignity:

Man doth seeke a triple perfection, first, a sensuall, consisting in those things which very life it selfe requireth either as necessary supplementes, or as beauties and ornaments therof; then an intellectuall, consisting in those things which none underneth man is either capable of or acquainted with; lastly a spirituall and divine, consisting in those things wherunto we tend by supernatural meanes here, but cannot here attaine unto them. (1.11.4)

The existence of a spiritual desire in man argues for the immortality of the soul, for "If the soule of man did serve onelye to geve him beinge in this life, then thinges appertayning unto this life woulde content him . . ." (1.11.4). Spiritual desire presupposes a reward, and reward in turn presupposes duties or works. Yet none of man's works can be pure enough to merit such a reward—hence the need for divine revelation: "God him self is the teacher of the truth, wherby is made knowen the supernaturall way of salvation and law for them to live in that shalbe saved" (1.11.5).

The bases of divine law are the theological virtues of faith, hope, and charity "without which there can be no salvation" (1.11.6), and they are found to be duties only in the received word of God. Laws divine are so both in origin and in subject matter, in that they have no basis in nature. Some divine laws reach further than laws of nature or positive law can reach, as do laws dealing with the human heart, and a few divine laws contradict what nature seems to teach, as for example the resurrection of the body. Yet Scripture is by no means limited to divine law, for it includes natural law and positive law as well.

As to the adequacy of the Scriptures to man's salvation, Hooker explains the idea both as a rational concept and as a matter of faith. A man cannot be trained as an orator unless he first can speak, nor does his training usually begin with the principles of grammar, a knowledge of these being assumed. So with Scripture: "the meaning cannot be simplye of all things that are necessarye, but all things that are necessarye in some certaine kinde or forme; as all things that are necessarye, and eyther could not at all, or could not easily be knowne by the light of naturall discourse; all things which are necessarye to be knowne that we may be saved, but knowne with presupposall of knowledge concerning certaine principles whereof it receaveth us already perswaded, and then instructeth us in all the residue that are necessarie" (1.14.1). And a necessary prior principle is a conviction of the sacred authority of Scripture, which Scripture itself cannot teach. Certain doctrines, e.g., the Trinity and Infant Baptism, are "in scripture no where to be found by expresse literall mention, only deduced they are out of scripture by collection" (1.14.2). This "collection" from Scripture through discourse Hooker would limit to what is *necessary*, not what may be conjectured or surmised.

Since some beliefs essential to salvation are beyond the reach of man's natural reason, a need for revelation becomes obvious. Since God saw fit to cause man to write down his Word for continuance and assurance, it is a reasonable conclusion that Scripture does contain all belief that is essential to man's salvation and that both Testaments contribute to this end. Scriptural law may build upon natural law, which to Hooker is likewise essential: "It sufficieth therefore that nature and scripture doe serve in such full sort, that they both joyntly and not severallye eyther of them be so complete, that unto everlasting felicitie wee neede not the knowledge of any thing more then these two, may easily furnish our mindes with on all sides..." (1.14.5).

Law and the Church. A point crucial in the controversy with the Puritans next arises: all categories of law—those of politic societies, of nations in dealing with each other, or of God expressed in Scripture—include both natural and positive laws. Positive laws may be subject to alteration, whereas natural laws are not; and from this Hooker proves that some of God's positive laws in Scripture are subject to alteration. "Positive lawes are either permanent or else changeable, according as the matter it selfe is concerning which they were first made" (1.15.1). Among alterable laws from Scripture are "the judicials which God gave unto the people of *Israell* to observe" (1.15.1). This precedent would seem to weaken the Puritan argument that scriptural law serves as an adequate basis for church polity.

Laws imposing specific religious duties, either from the Scriptures or by the society of the church, are all positive laws. God prescribed supernatural duties to the individual through the Gospel, which is eternal. The church is in part a society political, subject to laws derived from nature, and in part supernatural, subject to laws of worship prescribed by God and therefore unalterable. Positive laws revealed to man and to the church can be changed only by God. But not all law applicable to the church as a society is derived from divine revelation: "lawes that were made for men or societies or Churches, in regarde of theyr being such as they doe not always continue, but may perhaps be cleane otherwise a while after, and so may require to be otherwise ordered then before . . ." (1.15.3). Alteration of positive law applies to matters of church polity expressed in the Bible: "the whole lawe of rites and Ceremonies, although delivered with so great solemnitie, is notwithstanding cleane abrogated, in as much as it had but temporarie cause of Gods ordeyning it" (1.15.3). Hooker concludes this section with praise of Scripture as a source of wisdom to man, along with his reason and his perception.

Conclusion. The concluding section of book 1 offers summary and perspective. Hooker again lists the categories of law he has analyzed and defends the manner in which he first showed that all laws derive from God and then traced the kinds of law to their original causes. This approach, he maintains, teaches the force of laws and enables man to judge them reasonable, just, or righteous. The complexity of judging laws is increased because they are not entirely discrete: "seeing that our whole question concerneth the qualitie of Ecclesiasticall lawes, let it not seeme a labour superfluous that in the entrance thereunto all these severall kindes of lawes have beene considered, in as much as they all concurre as principles, they all have their forcible operations therein, although not all in like apparent and manifest maner" (1.16.1). Man should be sober and discreet in proceeding to weigh laws because they may have benefits not readily discernible and because all law derives ultimately from God.

The multiple kinds of law reinforce and support each other in a fundamental unity. The error of the Puritans is "to thinke that the only law which God hath appointed unto men in that behalfe is the sacred Scripture" (1.16.5). Men glorify God through sensory experience, through rational discourse, through their faith, and through obedience to laws of societies. The Puritans are essentially good men who do not take sufficient account of the types of laws and of the need for obedience: "Thus by following the law of private reason, where the law of publique should take place, they breede disturbance" (1.16.6).

To show that many laws affect one simple thing, Hooker uses the example of food. Man distinguishes objects as food through his senses, which he has in common with beasts. His reason tells him that he should be thankful to his Creator for the food he receives and should be moderate in eating. Divine law may endow certain foods with spiritual significance, and civil society may initiate laws regarding consumption of food. Further, a church may initiate positive laws regarding fasting. It follows that "to measure by any one kind of law all the actions of men were to confound the admirable order, wherein God hath disposed all lawes, ech as in nature, so in degree distinct from other" (1.16.7).

Book 2: Scripture as Sole Guide

In his second book, Hooker gives a sustained answer to the Puritans' position "that one onely lawe, the scripture, must be the rule to direct in all things..." (2.1.2). The book explores three major topics of controversy related to the subject of scriptural authority: (1) whether Scripture provides the sole guide to human actions (chapters 1–4), (2) whether negative arguments from Scripture always have binding force (chapters 5–6), and (3) whether human authority has binding moral force (chapter 7). In this book Hooker relies heavily upon theologians, taking one long quotation from Bishop Jewel, "the worthiest Divine that Christendome hath bred for the space of some hundreds of yeres..." (2.6.4).

Human Action. In refutation of the major argument for total reliance upon Scripture, Hooker devotes a chapter to each of four quotations from Thomas Cartwright. In taking the view that wisdom is derived solely from Scripture, Hooker says, the Puritans are defending too narrow a position, for the sources of wisdom are varied. He relies in this section upon historical fact, showing that Old Testament heroes attained wisdom without scriptural guidance. A man's wisdom is tested by his right action; and much right action is obviously free of scriptural influences. Some wisdom does indeed come from Scripture, some from nature, some from art, some from experience, some from heavenly inspiration, so that the sources of right action are rich and varied. Regarding the position that all of man's actions should glorify God, Hooker points out that God does not receive "any augmentation of glory at our hands" (2.2.1) and attempts to refute the Puritan view, expressed by Cartwright, by showing that the Apostle Paul could not have intended his words in 1 Corinthians 10:31 to apply to every human action:

We move, we sleepe, we take the cuppe at the hand of our freind, a number of thinges we oftentimes doe, only to satisfie some naturall desire, without present expresse, and actuall reference unto any commaundement of God. Unto his glory even these things are done which we naturally performe, and not onely that which morally and spiritually we doe.... But it doth not therefore follow that of necessitie we shall sinne, unlesse we expressely intend this in every such particular. (2.2.1)

During the early history of the church, infidels recognized the good works of Christians, even though they were ignorant of Scripture, and this recognition implies an ability in man to apprehend right action without direct guidance of the Bible. In Hooker's view what a person eats or drinks should be a matter of indifference so long as man acknowledges God's providence as the source of his bounty. The idea that one should seek guidance from Scripture on such particulars as eating seems extreme.

To assail another point of the Puritan position, he quotes Thomas Cartwright: *"that whatsoever is not of fayth, is sinne. But fayth is not but in respect of the worde of God. Therefore whatsoever is not done by the worde of God is sinne"* (2.4.1). "Faith," according to Hooker, refers to "some uttered worde, as the object of beliefe" (2.4.1). Extended beyond this, as in the syllogism of Cartwright, faith becomes belief in that which is experienced through senses and perceived by reason. Hooker urges that the Puritans modify their position that anything not done according to the Word of God is sin, maintaining that they should take into account indifferent things not prescribed but left to man's discretion and suggesting that the position would be better phrased: for "every action not commanded of God or permitted with approbation, faith is wanting, and for want of faith there is sinne" (2.4.3).

In most matters relevant to bodily needs, man is left to his own discretion and freedom of choice, unless he limits himself through a vow or promise or unless God institutes some law. It is unnecessary that the Bible prescribe every human action if one conceives of its message as liberating and not restricting; what the Bible does not forbid it permits, leaving man's discretion as a guide. If one exercises his discretion and makes his choices, then he is not to be convicted of sin. As an illustration of "things indifferent"—neither commanded nor prohibited by Scripture—Hooker cites a man seated at a table with a choice of several dishes before him. The individual may choose as he sees fit: "A hard case, that hereupon I should be justly condemned of sinne" (2.4.5). He invokes St. Augustine to demonstrate that belief in what is not contrary to Scripture may be acceptable and urges a second alteration in the Puritan position: "Let them therefore with Saint *Augustine* reject and condemne that which is not grounded either on the scripture, or on some reason not contrarie to scripture, and we are readie to give them our hands in token of friendlie consent with them" (2.4.7).

Negative Arguments. In the long Puritan controversy, the issue of negative arguments arose early and assumed importance. It represents the reverse of the medal whose obverse is inscribed, "Scripture as a guide to all action," for it proclaims that what is not sanctioned by Scripture may not be accepted. If Scripture contains no precedent, then the matter must be condemned and rejected, a kind of reasoning the Puritans found in writings of early theologians. When the church fathers used negative arguments from Scripture, as Hooker points out, they were speaking not of man's actions but of doctrine, matters of faith, and their position does not therefore support the Puritan argument of the Bible as the sole guide to all of man's actions. Hooker shows that passages from the fathers cited in support of the position are wrenched from context (Cyprian) or misinterpreted (Tertullian) or heretical (Tertullian after he had become a Montanist).

Turning to the position of negative arguments generally, Hooker acknowledges that certain ones from Scripture are compelling, especially when they concern God's specific instructions about matters of worship. To go beyond, as the Jews did in sacrificing to Baal, represents a serious offense. Relying on Jewel, Hooker shows that the church fathers used negative arguments drawn from Scripture and from other theologians, as well as from precedent. Freely acknowledging the strength of negative arguments, he asserts that "the question is not, whether an argument from scripture negatively may be good, but whether it be so generally good, that in all actions men may urge it" (2.6.4). The reference to negative arguments from nonscriptural authority leads Hooker to examine the Puritan position regarding human authority.

Human Authority.   On the issue of human authority Hooker recognizes the revolutionary potential of the Puritan argument: "For the scope of all their pleading against mans authoritie is, to overthrowe such orders, lawes, and constitutions in the Church, as depending thereupon if they should therfore be taken away, would peradventure leave neither face nor memorie of Church to continue long in the world, the world especially being such as now it is" (2.7.1). Cartwright had written that *"the authoritie of a man . . . holdeth neither affirmatively nor negatively"*; to Hooker, the Bible itself and common customs uphold man's authority in affairs of state and justice. The expertise of specialists, common consent, established tradition, and testimony all have force of authority. All truth derived from history rests upon the authority of man's testimony, and even negative human arguments of this kind can be strong. As for the reliability of human authority in divine matters of belief, Hooker makes two points: (1) The authority of man teaches belief in the infallibility of the Bible. (2) It is reasonable to believe that men can be so learned and inspired as to give reliable judgment in such matters.

Some matters of faith—the means of creation of man's soul, the perpetual virginity of Mary—are not fully clarified by the Bible, an ambiguity that causes perplexity among men. In the absence of infallible proof, the conclusions of learned men on those points might reasonably be granted some authority. Hooker shows a kind of preference for the authority of church councils, yet recognizes that no human authority can overrule Scripture.

The total rejection of human authority has pernicious consequences: "Thus much we see, it hath alreadie made thousandes so headstrong even in grosse and palpable errors, that a man whose capacitie will scarce serve him to utter five wordes in sensible maner, blusheth not in any doubt concerning matter of scripture to thinke his own bare *Yea*, as good as the *Nay* of all the wise, grave, and learned judgements that are in the whole world" (2.7.6). Even the disciples spoke respectfully of the scribes and asked Jesus for a ruling, and the normal manner of settling disputes is to seek some learned authority. Authority and proof from Scripture rely in part upon man's authority and wisdom, for these enable man to understand that scriptural passages actually support a particular argument. And the Puritan argu-

ment that their church discipline rests upon Scripture can be reduced
to this: "That *some thinges* which they maintaine, as far as *some men*
can *probably conjecture*, do *seeme* to have bene out of scripture *not
absurdly* gathered" (2.7.9).

Hooker concludes book 2 with a summary of his main arguments
and positions, accompanied by the heading, "A declaration what the
truth is in this matter." All of men's actions are either good or evil,
are in some sense voluntary—with or without deliberation. All good
ultimately derives from God, but men frame many of their actions
upon God's law of nature, not upon revelation, even though "nature
is no sufficient teacher what we shoulde doe that we may attaine unto
life everlasting" (2.8.3), and Scripture is essential for salvation. Further, some things commanded neither by Scripture nor by nature are
"of so great dignitie and acceptation with God, that most ample
reward in heaven is laid up for them" (2.8.4), such as self-sacrifice
and extraordinary services to others. Men's voluntary acts of this
kind are the basis for "whatsoever difference there is betweene the states
of Saincts in glory" (2.8.4). Scripture is perfect in providing man
truth and guidance in matters concerning salvation that are beyond
the power of reason, and truths of the Bible require no further addition or revelation. But Scripture is not intended as a replacement
for the "light of nature"; to consider it a guide for all actions would
have the consequence of involving all men in perplexity and anguish,
"For in every action of common life to find out some sentence cleerly
and infalliblie setting before our eyes what wee ought to doe, (seeme
wee in scripture never so expert) woulde trouble us more then wee
are aware" (2.8.6). Hooker keeps a middle course between Rome,
which teaches the necessity that Scripture be supplemented by tradition, and the Puritans, who see the Bible as the rule of all human
actions.

Book 3: Scripture and Polity

The third book of *Ecclesiastical Polity* refutes the Puritan claim
that Scripture provides the sole guidance for church polity, though
as one would assume, Hooker does much more than merely refute.
He clarifies his key terms "church" and "polity," explores both extreme and moderate Puritan positions on the question, defends the
role of reason in church polity, and anticipates some topics that he

will develop in later books, such as particular forms of worship and the status of the ministry. One remarkable characteristic of book 3 is the number of precedents and analogies drawn from biblical history to be used as evidence for his arguments; the book reveals the range and depth of Hooker's biblical knowledge and historical perspective.

"Church" and "Polity."   As he prepares to respond to a specific Puritan position, Hooker clarifies at the outset what he means by "church," and his definition differs from that which most Puritans of his time would have given. The church of Christ is one collective body or society, including all professing Christians on earth and all the saints of heaven. Though man can recognize the existence of the body, he cannot say with certainty who truly belongs and who does not, those in heaven being obscured from his sight and those on earth being persons whose soundness and sincerity as Christians cannot be weighed by human understanding. The visible church of this world has a historic division—the Jews before the coming of Christ and the Christians afterward professing *"One Lord, one faith, one baptisme"* (3.1.7).

In the world the visible mark of a Christian is the outward profession of belief in Christ sealed by baptism. Since man cannot determine the sincerity of others, those in the church who are Christians by external profession must be accepted as Christians. Excommunication may remove a person from Christian fellowship, but not from the church. Neither Luther nor any other reformer has established a new church, the essence of reform being to change and improve: "We hope therfore that to reforme our selves, if at anie time we have done amisse, is not to sever our selves from the Church we were of before. In the Church we were and we are so still" (3.1.10). To exclude professing Christians from the church is perilous, for it is as easy for man to deny one branch of the church as another. The church of Rome, though in need of reform, is a church still, and Calvin's opinion denying baptism to infants belonging to Catholic parents "doth seeme crased" (3.1.12).

Turning to the nature of the church, Hooker explains that his primary subject is the visible church on earth, which now is seen primarily as a "society": "the Catholike Church is . . . devided into a number of distinct societies, every of which is termed a Church within it selfe" (3.1.14). Examples of church societies are Rome, Corinth,

Ephesus, England, and each of these has "correspondent generall prop-erties," an important one being church polity. It would reasonably fol-low that since different churches or societies have varying polities, church government cannot be a matter essential to salvation. And Scripture, being essential for man's salvation, would not reasonably be expected to prescribe a uniform church polity. Hooker explains that he uses "Church-politie" instead of "church government" "be-cause it conteyneth both governement and also whatsoever besides belongeth to the ordering of the Church in publique" (3.1.14). It may be based upon what Scriptures reveal "or else as those thinges which men finde out by helpe of that light, which God hath given them unto that ende" (3.2.1). He charges that the Puritans cannot cite one church polity from history that has accorded fully with Scripture, nor do they defend their own as such, nor can they fully clarify what they derive explicitly from Scripture and what they infer.

Doctrine and Discipline.   Hooker rejects the Puritan position that doctrine (matters of faith) and discipline (polity) are insepar-able, both being necessarily of biblical origin. The early Puritans who attacked the Church of England proposed that *"Nothing ought to be established in the Church which is not commaunded by the worde of God"* (3.5.1), a position based upon their reading of Deuteronomy 4:2. They proceeded to find many things not commanded in the Word—the ring in marriage, the cross in baptism, kneeling at com-munion, laws of fast and abstinence, clerical offices. Hooker believes that the Puritans distorted the meaning of the Bible to further their own ends and asserts that application of their principle would affect all churches everywhere, even that during the time of the Apostles.

In an effort to demonstrate that the Bible leaves matters of polity to the discretion of the church itself, Hooker cites, from 1 Corinthians and Acts, four general canons of Paul concerning polity. He further argues that "the Church of the Jewes" (3.7.2) developed rules to regulate rites and ceremonies without the command of Scripture. His summary of the positions and precedents is apt and cogent:

Seeing therefore those canons doe bind as they are edicts of nature, which the *Jewes* observing as yet unwritten, and thereby framing such Churchorders, as in their law were not prescribed, are notwithstanding in that respect unculpable; it followeth that sundrie things may be lawfullie done in the Church, so as they be not done against the scripture, although no scripture doe commaund them, but the Church only following the light of reason, judge them to be in discretion meete. (3.7.2)

Hooker finds the Puritan position inconsistent and untenable. If Scripture provided all specific laws, there would be no need for the scriptural canons. Further, the Puritans profess that the church derives its particular laws from Scripture, when, in fact, they establish specific laws derived from the general canons of the Bible. Not only this—they disobey the laws of the Church of England on the grounds that they are not specifically written in the Bible and refuse to accept the right of the church to establish polity by "generall rules and canons" (3.7.4).

Authority of Reason. Among the Puritans some take a more moderate stance in which "commaunded in the word" becomes "grounded uppon the word." This position gives Hooker an opportunity to defend the role of reason in church polity. He lists and refutes six arguments against overreliance upon reason, which he says are the usual and common ones of the Puritans, some of the arguments being relevant to faith as well as to polity. He sees reason as much more efficacious in helping man accept, understand, and defend the Christian faith than inspiration or spirit. The apostles Peter and Paul themselves relied heavily upon reason to convert their audiences.

To institute laws for the church, the proper authority takes into account natural and positive law, the precedents provided by Scripture, and the judgments of reason. Hooker quotes St. Thomas Aquinas, the "greatest amongst the Schoole divines," to the effect that a human law, either civil or ecclesiastical, is a rule derived from the precepts of natural law through the process of reasoning. Hooker agrees with Aquinas's position: "*Humane lawes are measures* in respect of men whose actions they must direct, howbeit such measures they are, as have also their higher rules to be measured by, *which rules are two, the law of God, and the law of nature*" (3.9.2). He concludes from his examination that the second Puritan position admits the role of reason and that the only remaining issue is "what particulars the Church may appoint" (3.9.2). All can agree that man's reason discovers laws through the guidance of the natural law and that the laws of Scripture take priority.

The church having a legitimate right to make laws, and having made laws that are valid, man is bound to obey them: "the lawes thus made God himselfe doth in such sort authorize, that to despise them is to despise in them him" (3.9.3). In Hooker's chain of deduction, everything derives from God, if not directly, at least indirectly: "The author of that which causeth another thing to be, is author of that thing also, which thereby is caused. The light of naturall understanding wit and reason is from God. . . . He is the author of all that we thinke or doe by vertue of that light, which himselfe hath given" (3.9.3). The proper course for Christians thus includes obedience to the laws of God and man.

Alteration of Law. Laws of church polity, like other human laws, are changeable. Some laws may be instituted for a specified time, in accordance with man's judgment: "The nature of everie lawe must be judged of by the ende for which it was made, and by the aptnes of thinges therein prescribed unto the same end" (3.10.1). Reasons for some of God's laws are beyond man's understanding and therefore those laws may be changed only by God's will. Yet some laws of God were designed for ends which no longer exist (i.e., the ceremonial laws given through Moses) and thus have been abrogated. A more formidable argument arises when laws whose ends are still necessary and important are altered. Hooker defends this kind of alteration: "lawes though both ordeyned of God himselfe, and the end for which they were ordeined continuing, may notwithstanding cease, if by alteration of persons or times they be found unsufficient to attain unto that end" (3.10.4). This conclusion does not imply that man's judgment can better God's law, for "God never ordeyned any thing that could be bettered" (3.10.5). But some biblical ordinances have been changed for the better, because alterations of time and circumstance required change. Church polity may legitimately vary according to time and place, though Hooker recognizes that this kind of relativism undermines his position. As for the polity recommended by the Puritans, Hooker's relativism does not mean that he considers it on equal footing with the established polity: "Our perswasion is, that no age ever had knowledge of it but onely ours, that they which defend it devised it, that neither Christ nor his Apostles at any time taught it but the contrarie" (3.10.8). Still, he will not defend the Church of England as the *only* legitimate polity, rather as *a* legitimate polity.

He undertakes an analysis of the Puritan beliefs, based upon passages from the New Testament, that Christ established an unalterable polity. The Puritans had claimed that those who denied this position made Christ inferior to Moses, for Moses had left a polity. The feebleness of this argument Hooker makes apparent through an analogy to civil law and he goes on to point out specific differences between the times of Moses and Christ. Even with the extensive Mosaic Law, the Jews added many other laws as times and conditions required. The command of Paul to Timothy to keep the commandments refers not to the commandments of church polity but to preaching the word and remaining true to his calling; it, therefore, is no argument for a specific church polity.

In attempting to overturn established church polity and to replace it with one of their own making, the Puritans "have molested the Church with needelesse opposition" (3.11.19). Some functions of the church are forever unalterable but "Lawes of politie are lawes which appoint in what maner these duties shalbe performed" (3.11.20). The proper ones to perform the duties are the clergy, whose role the New Testament establishes: "Hereupon we hold that Gods clergie are a state which hath beene and will be, as long as there is a Church upon earth, necessarie by the plaine word of God himselfe; a state whereunto the rest of Gods people must be subject as touching things that appertaine to their soules health" (3.11.20). Anticipating positions developed in later books, Hooker notes that clergy rule over lay people and are ordered by ranks. Lawful practice will not permit every man to take it upon himself to speak with authority in the church and therefore a polity regulating admittance to clerical status is required.

The Puritans' argument that the Bible establishes a single polity in perpetuity is fallacious, and their argument that through Scripture they come to know the will of God in all its details appears to Hooker vain and presumptuous. Their polity advocates lay elders in the church, for which there is no precedent in the Bible, and a special status for widows, which has been removed since apostolic times.

An Aristotelian, deeply respectful of and influenced by the past, Hooker reveals in book 3 his substantial and pervasive debt to Aquinas and to scholasticism generally. But, as Arthur Ferguson points out, he differs from Aquinas in his view that the world is more diverse and complex than it seemed to Aquinas.[5] Hooker acknowledges, for example, the existence of national churches and legitimate variations of polity among them. Given the reality of the Elizabethan Settlement he had little other choice, but his vision of a church as a national society is no less genuine. It illustrates well a problem that arises with Hooker: his ideas, if pressed further than he takes them, involve some inconsistency and internal contradiction within his well-unified system. It has long been recognized that Hooker allows for variation of polity among the several national churches, whereas he makes no provision for variations *within* a national church.[6] He agrees with lessons from the *Book of Homilies*, that disobedience of the national polity amounts to disobedience of divine commands—cogent testimony of the powerful hold nationalism exerted upon intellectuals during the Renaissance.

Book 4: Orders, Rites, and Ceremonies

In book 4, Hooker refutes the objection that the Church of England *"is corrupted with popish orders rites and ceremonies"* which in the Puritan view should be removed in accordance with the practice of other reformed churches. Throughout, Hooker responds to specific passages from the writings of Thomas Cartwright, whom he cites extensively and repeatedly. Of the three subjects—orders, rites, and ceremonies—Hooker chooses to consider objections primarily to ceremonies. In the fourteen chapters, he answers five major objections to ceremonies in the Church of England, four of the objections being treated in one chapter each. The second objection, "that so many of them [ceremonies] are the same which the Church of Rome useth," receives eight chapters, amounting to more than one third of the book.

The introduction points out that moderate Puritans like Cartwright are able to make a distinction bewween minor and major points of polity and explains that the book will concern major and general objections to church polity. Historically, there has always been a church to prescribe how the mission of edifying man in faith is carried out, and for this mission, Hooker says, speech alone is not adequate. Added ceremony has always been deemed proper, since things that can be seen impress the mind more deeply toward understanding and acceptance than spoken words. Not realizing this, the Puritans too easily discount the importance of ceremonies. Some ceremonies of the church—the Lord's Supper and Baptism—are sacraments; other significant ceremonies—e.g., ordination—are only "as sacraments." Hooker defines "sacrament" at this point, a definition important to his later work: "Sacraments are those [ceremonies] which are signes and tokens of some generall promised grace, which alwaies really

descendeth from god unto the soul that duly receiveth them..."
(4.1.4).

The Apostolic Model. In answer to the objection that the church has departed from practices of apostolic times, Hooker urges that the Bible is none too clear about what early practices were, since the New Testament gives information about matters of polity when there is need or reason, not otherwise. Further, to limit church order and rites to the era of the Apostles is to rule out change based upon external conditions. Hooker has no trouble demonstrating that during their bondage the Jews followed a different external order of worship from the order used after they had established their own nation. So the church, during times of persecution, may baptize people in brooks, but the rite should be performed under more dignified surroundings once the church has been recognized by society. Conditions have changed since the Apostles' time, so that changes in polity are natural and desirable.

The Precedent of Rome. When he takes up the argument that the church still follows the example of Rome too closely, Hooker demonstrates once again his antipathy to extremism. Through their scripturalism, the Puritans are able to denounce as "popish" everything in the church which they do not find sanctioned by the Bible. Hooker quotes Cartwright to the effect that whatever Rome follows, not taken from the Bible but not opposed to it, should be abandoned. Against this view Hooker takes the position that whatever is sound ought not to be abandoned. In developing this argument he gives a thorough account of the rationale for the Puritan position. Cartwright pointed out that God seems to have purged Jewish worship of all Egyptian influence because the closest neighbor likely presents the greatest temptation toward idolatry. Cartwright argued through analogy that reformed churches might follow the precedent of the Turks more safely than that of the Catholics. Indeed, the cure for papacy to the Puritan is like that for paganism presented by Tertullian: Christians should do the opposite in matters indifferent.

Hooker charges the Puritans with using their accusations of popery as a kind of propaganda to turn adherents from the Church of England. When they are thus charged, Puritan intellectuals profess to attack only rites, orders, and ceremonies known to be profitless, a specious response because they know the church has retained only those considered profitable. On this question, Hooker reveals what Burke calls an inclination to preserve, which in his thought is strong:

"If they thinke that we ought to prove the ceremonies commodious which we have retained, they do in this pointe very greatly deceave them selves. For in all right and equitie that which the Church hath received and held so long for good, that which publique approbation hath ratified, must cary the benefite of presumption with it to be accompted meete and convenient. . . . The burthen of proving doth rest on them" (4.4.2). Again the Puritans are cast in the roles of plaintiffs or defendants, and the weight of lawful sanction rests with established practice.

Some customs and rites held in common with Rome spring from a common ancient source; moreover, some reformed churches, including that of Geneva, follow customs and rites which English Puritans have denounced as popish. Concerning the analogy to Egypt, Hooker argues that it is unclear how great a separation there actually was and that the Jews and early Christians on occasion followed paganism in matters generally considered noncontroversial. As for curing contraries by contraries, or straightening a bent stick by bending it as far as possible in the opposite direction, Hooker introduces a similar analogy to show that an unaccaptable result might be achieved: "He that will take away extreme heate by setting the body in extremitie of cold, shal undoubtedly remove the disease, but together with it the diseased too" (4.8.1). Examples of Christians who have gone to an extreme to deny Rome are the Arians in Poland, who deny the Trinity. Hooker believes that the learned Puritans like Cartwright denounce the extremes of popery at first but intend to return to a moderate position after they have prevailed.

A more serious facet of the objection raised by Cartwright—one which Hooker was aware of but tended to underrate—was that if the rites and ceremonies of the church resembled those of Rome, it would be much easier for Roman dominance to return. Cartwright had made this point emphatically, citing Martin Bucer as its source. The existence of bishops, for example, would make it relatively easy for a Catholic ruler to exert his will through the church hierarchy, as Queen Mary had done, and to the Puritans a repetition of this episode loomed as a dreadful prospect. Hooker dismisses as mere petulence the desire of the Puritans to root out all remnants of previous practice. Though he recognizes the logic of Bucer's view that the church by rites in common with Rome might make the reestablishment of Catholicism easier, he deems it essentially irrelevant:

as we denie not but this may be true, so being of two evils to choose the lesse, we hold it better, that the friends and favourers of the Church of Rome should be in some kind of hope to have a corrupt religion restored, then both we and they conceive just feare, least under colour of rooting out Poperie, the most effectuall meanes to beare up the state of religion be remooved, and so a way made eyther for Paganisme, or for extreme barbaritie to enter. (4.9.3)

Again he seeks to defend a moderate course between the extremes.

Those Puritans who grieve because of the popish practices of the church must endure them until the church changes them. Meanwhile they may take heart from the example of the church of Geneva, which retains customs found to be odious by Puritans in England. For the Puritans' grief the most effective medicine is not to alter the church but rather to change "that perswasion which they have concerning the same" (4.10.1).

The Puritans regard church polity in things indifferent as diseased and ask the church to reform simply on the authority of their word, but "the world hath not as yet had so great experience of their arte in curing the diseases of the Church..." (4.10.2). The difficulty in applying their admonitions that the church should be opposite to Rome in things indifferent Hooker clarifies through illustration. The Puritan axiom would require the church to use leavened bread for the Eucharist because Catholics use unleavened bread—"let them imagin a reformed Church in the Citie of *Venice*, where a Greeke Church and a Popish both are. And when both these are equallie neere, let them consider what the third shall doe. Without eyther leavened or unleavened bread, it can have no sacrament..." (4.10.3). The principle which the Puritans uphold might become impossible to apply.

The Jewish Model. The third major point which Hooker refutes relates to those ceremonies from the church of Rome particularly objectionable because they came originally from the Jews. Alleged reasons for rejecting these are the Jews' opposition to Christ and the abrogation of the law through the Gospel. These in themselves are not strong reasons, for "Jewish ordinances had some things naturall, and of the perpetuitie of those things no man doubteth" (4.11.4). Furthermore, the early church permitted Jewish converts to practice some ceremonies of their religion. When Christians argued that Gentiles converted to Christianity had to observe the Mosaic Law, the Council of Jerusalem settled the question. How much Jewish ceremony was accepted remains unclear; it is clear that the Apostles thought that Gentiles should observe some Jewish law and custom, and Hooker cites New Testament passages in support of Jewish law based upon custom or nature.

He then develops a subtle point regarding Jewish law and ceremonies. New Testament passages show that these were not immediately rejected and abandoned by Christians, and, indeed, the Mosaic law should not be entirely abandoned. Nothing better illustrates Hooker's conservative, irenic inclination than his judgment of Jewish rites: "throughout all the writings of the auncient fathers we see that the words which were do continue; the only difference is, that whereas before they had a literall, they now have a metaphoricall use, and are as so many notes of remembrance unto us, that what they did signifie in the letter, is accomplished in the truth" (4.11.10). Even though Jewish rites are not commanded, neither are they forbidden, and they may be beneficial in that they nurture an awareness in Christians of the continuity of providence.

The Issue of Scandal. The fourth major point has to do with the Puritans' denunciation of religious rites taken from the church of Rome which they assert to be scandalous. Hooker explains what "scandal" means: "Men are scandalized when they are moved, led, and provoked unto sinne" (4.12.2). He cites some examples of scandalous rites from various heretical movements that had as their purpose subversion of orthodox doctrines. But he argues that the Roman rites of "Crossing at Baptisme, of kneeling at the Eucharist, of using Wafer-cakes, and such like" (4.12.4) cannot be considered scandalous in themselves. Even some customs whose purpose was originally in opposition to Christianity—as, for example, naming months and days from pagan myths—may in time be regarded as innocuous.

The Puritans charge that such ceremonies, while not forbidden in the Bible, are not commanded, and expediency requires that the church abandon them. They cite Paul's statement that he abstains from foods forbidden to the Jews, though not to him, because a violation of their custom might cause Jewish Christians to reject the faith. Hooker illustrates why the analogy in this case is unsound and promises to defend these particular ceremonies elsewhere (book 5), weighing reasons that have been stated against them.

The Reformed Model. The final point made by the Puritans is that the Church of England has not been so quick to rid itself of traditional ceremonies as other reformed churches, the church being bound to follow reformed examples. Against numerous reasons and precedents from Cartwright, Hooker maintains that it is doubtful how far the church should follow the practice of other reformed churches. The Puritan position that all churches should be as much alike as possible means, says Hooker, that they be exactly alike, for it is possible for any church to change rites and ordinances left discretionary by the Bible. To him this objective seems untenable, and he cites passages from Gregory and Augustine in justification of some variety among churches, the passage from Augustine having had the support of Calvin. Unless ceremonies are ruled upon by a general council, then churches, as societies, remain free to make their own rules regarding ceremonies and rites. Hooker would acknowledge the authority of a general council over ceremony, but the imitation of individual churches he rejects. To the Puritan position that older reformed churches should become patterns for the newer ones, Hooker cites the church in apostolic times as a refutation, explaining that the first churches provided examples, not law. The Church of England is not obligated to condemn the ceremonies of others or to abandon its own.

The conclusion of book 4 is a kind of justification of the general positions of the church regarding ceremonies as they relate to Catholic and reformed churches. Hooker believes that in its proceeding regarding rites, forms, and ceremonies the Church of England has been reasonable. Even though it becomes necessary to change laws through their own imperfection, through a change of conditions, through original mistakes in passing them, any change diminishes the willingness of men to obey laws because change implies an admission either of ineffectuality or of error. Hooker acknowledges that the Apostles who had the guidance of the Holy Spirit, which the Puritans lack, altered Jewish and pagan law. In modern times, laws should be changed only when those who advocate the changes can logically demonstrate that change is necessary. It is not sufficient to profess that a law is useless or ineffectual, for the weight of tradition and authority fall on the side of the law: "As for arbitrarie alterations, when lawes in them selves not simply bad or unmeete are changed for better and more expedient; if the benefit of that which is newly better devised bee but small, sith the custome of easines to alter and change is so evill, no doubt but to beare a tollerable soare is better then to venter on a daungerous remedie" (4.14.2). In the matter of reforming rites and ceremonies, Hooker characterizes the course and

proceeding of the Church of England as one of "reasonable moderation."

He ends book 4 with a passage praising those civil rulers who did
the most to reform the church: Henry VIII, Edward VI or *"Edward
the Saint,"* and Queen Elizabeth, "a most glorious starre" (4.14.7),
whose efforts to further reformation abroad he praises. To Hooker,
the history of the church from the time of Henry VIII implies that
it has enjoyed divine favor and guidance.

Chapter Four
Ecclesiastical Polity,
Book 5:
Solemn and
Serviceable Worship

In an appendix to the fourth book of *Ecclesiastical Polity,* Hooker called the reader's attention to errata in the text and explained why he was publishing the first four books separately. He had not thought it wise to delay publication until the entire work was complete, and the general nature of the first four books made it desirable for the reader to consider them earlier. When in 1597 book 5 appeared alone, it was nearly one and one-half times as long as the first four books and preface combined. Publication was again by John Windet, the text being a copy transcribed by Benjamin Pullen, John Churchman's servant and Hooker's amanuensis. Hooker himself carefully supervised the printing, and the printer's copy, which includes numerous corrections and additions in his own hand, is now in the Bodleian Library.[1] The manuscript bears the approving signature of John Whitgift, archbishop of Canterbury, to whom Hooker dedicated the work.

Book 5 undertakes a defense of all the major specific rites, ceremonies, and orders of the Church of England in an effort to show that they are reasonable. Hooker seemingly overlooks nothing, as he examines Puritan objections to every section of the authorized prayer book and the ordinal. To some extent the organization follows that of the official manual of worship. Orientation toward the outward form of worship permits Hooker to avoid moving deeply into theological controversy and to postpone consideration of vexing questions of authority within the church.

He seeks to defend all the public duties of the church from the charge of superstition and the ministry from the charge of corruption. The book includes eighty-one chapters, compared with sixteen in book 1 and eight in book 2. Its organization is not readily apparent, but the major groupings can be ascertained from Hooker's list of "Matter contained" at the outset. The first ten chapters deal with generalities—distinctions between true religion and superstition, four axioms to apply in religious controversy, and one additional rule. The four axioms become premises in Hooker's deductive arguments in defense of public worship. Chapters 11–17 deal with church buildings, and chapters 18–22 concern preaching and reading from the Bible—that is, the role of the church as teacher. There follows a large section (chapters 23–49) on prayer in all its forms. The sacraments of Baptism and the Eucharist are the subjects of chapters 50–68, and chapters 69–75 concern other rites and observances of the church, such as festival days and the burial service. The concluding group of chapters (76–81) represents a defense of the ministry. The book, then, concerns seven major topics: (1) true religion and axioms supporting it, (2) church buildings, (3) preaching and reading, (4) prayer, (5) sacraments, (6) other rites, and (7) the ministry.

Dedication

In the dedication to Whitgift, Hooker acknowledges his respect for ecclesiastical authority and reflects his conservative position on law. He reviews some of the main points of controversy with the Puritans, but argues that in the entire history of the church the great controversies have been those concerning the nature of Christ and the primacy of Rome, so that by comparison the current controversy seems almost insignificant. Some opponents of the Puritans have been content to argue only matters of jurisdiction, but, Hooker explains, he has attempted an analysis of all Puritan objections, on the example of his patron: "Notwithstanding led by your Graces example my selfe have thought it convenient, to wade thorough the whole cause, following that method which searcheth the truth by the causes of truth" (Ded., 3).[2] Whitgift himself had earlier produced a tome refuting all the Puritan objections, though with a far different organization, and the fifth book clearly reveals Hooker's heavy debt to Whitgift. Perhaps a majority of his detailed defenses of public worship had been made before by the archbishop.

He justifies a lengthy defense at this time because the Puritans are a dangerous threat to society in their appeal for support, for "in Religion al men presume themselves interested alike" (Ded., 5) and in religious disputes men's emotions (passions) overrule their reason. In the preface to books 1–4, his chief example of the irrational in religion was the Anabaptists of Meunster; here he uses the examples of William Hacket, Edmund Coppinger, and Henry Arthington, fanatics who proclaimed themselves liberators and rebelled against the queen in 1591. Their notorious acts occurred in London and were a source of embarrassment to the moderate Puritans. Hooker refers to them as "poore seduced creatures" who became overpowered by their affection for Puritan discipline and their conviction of God's special guidance until their recklessness left them "in the ende an example for head-strong and inconsiderate zeale . . ." (Ded., 6).

In attempting to undermine ecclesiastical authority, the Puritans are allied with the writer of the Marprelate tracts; they do not wish merely "to reforme [church] ceremonies, but seeke farther to erect a popular authoritie of Elders, and to take away Episcopal jurisdiction" (Ded., 8), thus to subvert what Samuel Johnson calls the grand principle of subordination. In their efforts to undermine and overturn the bishops they have had the support of some in power who sought to advance their "odious and corrupt dealings in secular affaires" more easily. The remedy of churchmen thus under attack is wisdom tempered by innocent meekness, not wisdom set sharp to defend the clergy but rather that which shows how the established church remains beneficial to all. The dedication expresses a hope for resolution of the controversy and concludes with expressions praising the queen.

Axioms of Religion

Book 5 begins by asserting the importance of true religion to the individual and to society. Hooker agrees with the Puritans that true religion and faithful service to God are the main sources of virtuous action in any society, and he believes that justice is impossible without piety. For piety promotes in man both zeal and fortitude. Always the moderate, he will not argue that virtue cannot exist without true religion, yet religion does represent a powerful support. Whereas men agree that their best effects are inspired by religion, or by those faiths nearest the true one, some good effects are possible from any religion, even paganism, as Hooker shows by drawing examples from the Romans. If a man chooses the wrong religion, he is still better off than if he chose no religion: "They that love the religion which they profess may have fayled in choise, but yeat they are sure to reape what benefitt the same is able to afforde..." (5.1.4). Still, "all true vertues are to honor true religion as theire parente, and all well ordered common-weales [are] to love her as theire chiefest staye" (5.1.5).

To any nation the greatest danger comes from atheism, which denounces all religions as false. The atheist sees religion as an obstacle to his main motive in life, "a resolved purpose of minde to reape in this worlde what sensuall profitt or pleasure soever the world yealdeth, and not to be barred from any whatsoever meanes availeable thereunto" (5.2.1). This causes atheists to ignore the truth, to scoff at religion, and to grow stronger through contention. Seeing that religion has a place in politics, the atheist concludes that it "is a meere politique devise, forged purposelie to serve for that use" (5.2.3). Yet the real political use of religion is to serve as an inward check on man's inclination toward evil, as civil law serves as an external check. Hooker has read his Machiavelli, and the counsel to the ruler regarding religion leaves him cold because a rational effort to establish religion for political motives represents a cynical disregard of the truth.

Superstition stands at a distance from atheism as an opposite extreme, its causes being excessive zeal or excessive fear. Uncontrolled zeal is a dangerous threat, for it "useth the rasor many times with such eagernes, that the verie life of religion it selfe is thereby hazarded, through hatred of tares the corne in the feilde of God is pluckt up" (5.3.1). Unbridled fear clouds the reason and prompts in man a desperate effort to please God, with the result that almost any form of worship which holds promise becomes acceptable. Superstition has made itself felt during the history of the church through heresies and through excessive religious rites and ceremonies. Now the Church of England itself stands accused of being "stained with superstition," and Hooker judges that the attacks of the Puritans against practices regarded as expressions of reverence may confuse and trouble some who are unaccustomed to religious controversy. Thus he undertakes to defend the particulars of external worship: "Sollemne and serviceable worship we name, for distinction sake, whatsoever belongeth to the Church or publique societie of God by way of externall adora[ti]on" (5.4.3).

As guides or axioms for the defense of "Sollemne and serviceable worship" he develops four general propositions, "to serve as principles whereby to worke" (5.5.1). Having considered and rejected five Puritan principles in the preceding book, Hooker is ready to present his own axioms. His first is extremely complex, both in form and in applications. While no church can be perfect in its worship, perfection requiring infinite wisdom, the church should outwardly reflect man's internal striving toward God and should also reflect "a sensible excellencie, correspondent to the majestie of him whome we worship" (5.6.2), two factors requiring dignity and elevation. His first proposition, then, concerns the acceptability of ceremonies: "in thexternall forme of religion such thinges as are apparentlie, or can be sufficientlie proved effectuall and generallie fitt to set forwarde godlines, either as betokeninge the greatenes of God, or as beseeminge the dignitie of religion, or as concurringe with cœlestiall impressions in the mindes of men, maie be reverentlie thought of..." (5.6.2). This proposition better illustrates Hooker's inclination for being all-inclusive than for driving sharp distinctions, for it is so comprehensive as to justify almost anything. And as to its precision, what were the Puritans to make of "cœlestiall impressions"?

A second axiom is developed on the basis of human nature—the accepted principle that wisdom and wise counsel derive from age. There is an easy analogy of correspondence from men to institutions. Even the wisest men are not fully accepted by their societies until long after their deaths, the world being unwilling to believe that anyone can add very much to the wisdom of the past: "In which consideration there is cause why we should be slow and unwillinge to chaunge without verie urgent necessitie the ancient ordinances rites and longe approved customes of our venerable predecessors" (5.7.3). Hooker's second proposition is thus that "in thinges the fittnes whereof is not of it selfe apparent nor easie to be made sufficientlie manifest unto all, yeat the judgment of antiquitie concurringe with that which is receyved may induce them to thinke it not unfitt, who are not able to alleage any knowne waightie inconvenience which it hath, or to take any strong exception against" (5.7.4). The effect of this axiom appears to be that established practices in the church will be accepted, unless opponents can provide compelling arguments against them.

The third axiom is a kind of complement to the second, for it concerns changes in the positive laws of the church. Whereas the church reveres ancient tradition and practices, it is nevertheless an undying institution, and as such it has authority to make positive laws regarding its own functions, though not laws relating to doctrine, which does not change. Members are obligated to obey those laws and to refrain from measuring them through their private judgments. Hooker's third proposition, somewhat lengthy, stresses the authority of the church and the obedience men owe it:

> where neither the evidence of anie law divine, nor the streingth of anie invincible argument otherwise found out by the light of reason, nor anie notable publique inconvenience doth make against that which our own lawes ecclesiasticall have although but newlie instituted, for the orderinge of these affaires, the verie authoritie of the Church it selfe, at the least in such cases, maie give so much credit to her own lawes, as to make theire sentence touchinge fittnes and conveniencie waightier then anie bare and naked conceipt to the contrarie; especiallie in them who can owe no lesse then childlike obedience, to hir that hath more then motherlie power. (5.8.5)

Thus Hooker postulates that a church as a society has the power and authority to legislate and that its laws, therefore, require obedience.

In the final axiom Hooker deals with more subtle distinctions, the difference between law and equity or between law and right. Nothing is more uniform than the law of nature, and yet sometimes, for reasons not understood, nature's law is suspended. Similarly, laws of human action are alterable, according to the circumstance, as when St. Paul threw corn into the sea in an effort to preserve human lives (Acts 29:38). Laws and rules must in their application bend to necessities, permitting under the proper conditions actions which otherwise would be forbidden. Because laws are general, all laws imply exceptions, permitting dispensations, exemptions, and immunities. Yet in ecclesiastical law as in civil law, no man has the right to consider himself an exception, because each man will find it natural to interpret the law according to his own benefit. It follows that any society needs a body of men to interpret its laws and to decide cases involving equity. Hooker's final proposition seems almost self-evident: "we lastlie require that it maie not seeme harde, if in cases of necessitie, or for common utilities sake, certain profitable ordinances sometime be released, rather then all men allwaies strictlie bound to the generall rigor thereof" (5.9.5).

As an addendum to the axioms, he attaches a rule, indicating what is not permitted—men's private reason in ecclesiastical affairs. Against the collective wisdom of the church, the private will of man should not prevail, for if the individual truly had private inspiration from God, he could convince others either through performing miracles

or through "stronge and invincible remonstrance of sound reason . . ."
(5.10.1).

Church Buildings

The portion of book 5 concerning *"Places for the publique service of God"* (chapters 11–18) is the briefest of this long book, and it may be informative to see how Hooker applies his axioms. Each serves as a major premise in a deductive argument, usually an enthymeme with the major premise left for the reader to supply. One may identify the axioms to the rest of the argument by number, even when, as is usual, Hooker does not state them. In explaining the solemnity and dignity of appointed places of worship, he reviews the question historically from the Old Testament. Here it is well to recall that for Hooker terms like "nature," "law," and "church" have exceedingly broad meanings, the Jews of the Old Testament being in his view a part of the church. Thus they built magnificent temples at God's command (axiom 1) and their activity serves as a kind of precedent for the church (axiom 2). Hooker shows that there is a kind of parallel between the Jews and the Christians since they built costly places of worship in times when religion enjoyed the support of the nation and its rulers, whereas in adverse times the places of public worship were simpler. As he develops the point, he makes it clear that he believes the church fortunate because it has inherited costly edifices dedicated to worship and he is offended by the iconoclastic spirit of the Puritans who denounce the buildings as places of idolatry and seek to have them destroyed (implying his rule against private interpretation).

Answering a Puritan objection to ceremonies at laying the cornerstone and dedicating churches, Hooker regards the issue as only of minor importance, but he argues precedents to defend the ceremonies (axiom 2). Moreover, the ceremony itself lends dignity and promotes godliness (axiom 1). Following past practices, the Church of England sanctifies or hallows churches, "In which action other solemnities then such as are decent and fit for that purpose we approve none" (5.12.6) (axiom 1). As for naming churches after angels and saints, which the Puritans denounced as superstitious, Hooker cites the approval of St. Augustine as precedent (axiom 2) and points to reasons promoting godliness (axiom 1).

He defends the form of the church against the Puritan charge that

it resembles a Jewish temple by arguing that, their ends being the
same, certain similarities are to be expected (axiom 2), but he points
to several differences in detail. He defends, largely through precedent and analogy, the sumptuousness of churches, another objection
made by Puritans. If kings are to have elaborate palaces and castles,
should God not have elaborate and ornate temples? (axiom 1). A
fitting analogy for Hooker between church and state—but it ignores
the matter of how far some Puritans had gone toward rejecting the
idea of the church as a body politic comparable to the state. Hooker
does acknowledge that the church in its nonobligatory pomp must not
neglect its obligation to charitable works. Citing numerous precedents,
he admits that magnificence and dignity in church buildings are not
necessary for man to worship God aright, but argues that they do
increase in man those "cœlestiall impressions" in the mind (axiom 1):
"manifest notwithstandinge it is, that the verie majestie and holines
of the place, where God is worshipped, hath *in regarde of us* great
vertue force and efficacie, for that it serveth as a sensible help to stirre
up devotion, and *in that respect* no doubt *bettereth* even our holiest
and best actions in this kinde" (5.16.2).

The final issue he explores is the Puritan charge that the church
buildings, having previously served the purposes of idolatry (i.e., having been scenes for Mass), ought to be razed. Hooker agrees that
idolatry is serious, particularly in view of God's punishment of that
sin in the Bible, but the analogy made by the Puritans, he says, does
not apply. The analogy to Canaan in Deuteronomy 12 explains God's
wrath over idolatry, yet "It doth not appointe in what forme and
manner *we ought* to punish the synne of idolatrie *in all others*"
(5.17.4). Moreover, the Jews were receiving from God a new law,
and the historical analogy to the Reformation is not quite adequate:
"In this case we are to reteine as much, in the other as little of former
thinges as we may" (5.17.5). The erroneous worship in the churches
of England has been removed by law (axiom 3) and the buildings
are conveniently framed for the worship of God (axiom 1). God's
commandment in the Old Testament to the Jews concerning the
destruction of idolatrous temples was specific and limited and therefore does not apply to Christian churches.

Preaching and Reading

Hooker turns in the next major division to the responsibility of
providing public instruction in the knowledge of God. He defines the

instruction of the church as "preaching," but he uses the term broadly enough that it includes almost all kinds of instruction. The church carries out its preaching function by publishing and explaining the Scriptures, by explicating "the mysteries which lye hid therein" (5.19.1). Through public reading of the Bible, the church "preacheth onlie *as a wittnesse*" (5.19.2), and since fidelity is required of witnesses, this consideration gets Hooker into the question of the reliability of translations. Typically, he takes a moderate position, recognizing that the translation must steer between the literal and a paraphrase. He defends the reading of the Bible during service as modeled upon ancient practice, as a part of the liturgy—itself based upon ancient practice and therefore acceptable. Defending the use of Old Testament Apocrypha, he traces the controversies regarding readings during church service and the rulings of ancient councils. Historical evidence supports readings from the Apocrypha, though Hooker clearly has some personal reservations about the practice.

When he considers preaching of sermons, he explains that the meaning Puritans normally attach to "preaching" rules out reading from any text. Hooker asserts to the contrary that preaching is not limited to sermons and defends the position that public reading of Scriptures is as efficacious toward salvation as preaching. The church's care in preserving Scripture, in testifying to its authority, in having it read to reveal the truths of the Bible—all suggest the power of Scripture to lead men to salvation. Hooker directs his attack against arguments by the Puritans that sermons are more conducive to salvation than the Bible, particularly their argument which says that none can be saved by reading alone. The Gospel's admonition to preach does not imply that the church should teach through sermons only. Much less can the Puritans attribute to their sermons an authority equal to that of sermons recorded in the New Testament, for sermons are the work of men. Examining the positive claims put forth by the Puritans in support of sermons, Hooker finds either gross exaggeration or the misapplication of some biblical text in support of those claims. He believes that the Bible approves both reading and preaching and that neither represents an exclusive way to salvation.

Essential truths of the Bible are not so obscure that a layman can discover them only with help from a preacher: "The man which readeth the word of God the word it selfe doth pronounce blessed, if he also observe the same" (5.22.15). Some Puritans believed that in many parishes throughout England all the souls were lost because the clergy did not preach. Hooker's response includes the following: "We hold it safer a great deale and better to give them incouragement; to put them in minde that it is not the deepnes of theire knowledge, but the singlenes of theire beliefe which God accepteth . . ." (5.22.17). For the remainder of this section, he turns his arguments largely against the Puritans' logic and definitions, charging that they refuse to define "good preachinge," "good preacher," or "good sermon." He clearly recognizes the appeal of sermons to the audience and does not reject the sermon as one form of preaching.

Prayer

The section on prayer begins with a discussion of its purposes and turns to the ancient practice of assembling people for prayer, showing that public prayer promotes godliness. Hooker makes public prayer synonymous with common prayer, a solemn service conducted in a house of worship, led by a virtuous, godly minister devoted to service. As might be expected, Hooker lays heavy stress on the historical precedent in defense of a common church liturgy:

But of all helpes for due performance of this service, the greatest is that verie sett and standinge order it selfe, which framed with common advise hath both for matter and forme prescribed whatsoever is herein publiquely don. No doubt from God it hath proceeded and by us it must be acknowledged a worke of his singular care and providence, that the Church hath evermore held a prescript forme of common prayer. . . . So that if the liturgies of all ancient Churches throughout the world be compared amongst them selves, it may be easilie perceaved they had all one originall mould. . . . (5.25.4)

In this context "public prayer," "common prayer," and "liturgy" become synonymous, referring to the prescribed public service which Hooker takes pains to defend. Against the official liturgy the Puritans expressed a preference for private and extemporaneous individual prayer. While acknowledging that the more moderate Puritans find little serious objection to the liturgy, Hooker reviews a long list of charges against it. He proceeds to a few of them in detail—for example, the Puritan complaints that the service is too close to Catholic liturgy and that the minister wears improper vestments. He quotes at length from Puritan writings on vestments, pointing out inconsistencies in the arguments. Significantly, he sees the entire vestrian controversy as an important test of the Puritan ministers' willingness to obey lawful authority. He considers and answers specific Puritan objections to the following: gestures during the service, movements of the minister and congregation, the simplicity and length of the service, frequent short prayers, intermingling of lessons and prayers, prayers for temporal things, repetition of the Lord's Prayer, and repetition of the minister's words by the congregation.

When he comes to a consideration of psalms and hymns, he responds to the Puritans' objections to music and to interlocution, i.e., responses from all or part of the audience in unison. Few passages in Hooker suggest any degree of mysticism, yet when he defends the power of music, he reveals a sense of mystery:

And that there is such a difference of one kinde from another wee neede no proofe but our own experience, in as much as we are at the hearinge of some more inclyned unto sorrowe and heavines; of some, more mollified and softned in minde; one kind apter to staie and settle us, another to move and stirre our affections; there is that draweth to a mervelous grave and sober mediocritie, there is also that carryeth as it were into ecstasies, fillinge the minde with an heavenlie joy and for the time in a maner severinge it from the bodie. (5.38.1)

Perceiving the power of music, Hooker has no doubt that it can promote godliness. He grants that it does not much edify the understanding, yet it does edify the affection, "because therein it worketh much" (5.38.3).

Regarding prayers "wherein the people and the minister answere one an other by course," he has no difficulty showing that the practice had been in use in Christendom for approximately twelve hundred years. Historical precedent serves also to defend litanies, the Athanasian Creed, and the Gloria Patrie. In defense of the creed, he gives a thorough account of the Arian controversy, explaining the prominent and praiseworthy role of Athanasius in defense of orthodoxy. He seems to believe that the main benefit of the Gloria Patrie is in strengthening belief in the Trinity. Against the Puritan argument that the Arian controversy is no longer a threat, Hooker argues that its contribution to the service ought to be retained, for ancient heresies are showing themselves once again in the world.

Though most of their criticism is directed at excesses, the Puritans found one omission from the Book of Common Prayer—prayers of thanksgiving. Hooker explains that prayers of thanksgiving for deliverance from calamities are prescribed by the church as needed and are made at special ceremonies. But he goes on to point out that the Puritans would not be satisfied if the church included such prayers, for they argue against the Prayer Book as a whole, all prayers included. Here he indicates, as he does from time to time, that for some of the Puritans the criticisms are only tactics; they have larger objectives in mind all the while: "The truth is they wave in and out, no way sufficiently grounded, no way resolved what to thinke speake or write, more then onlie that because they have taken it upon them they must (no remedie now) be opposite" (5.43.5).

The final objections against the Book of Common Prayer concern the wording of five brief passages which the Puritans regard as unsound doctrine or inappropriate. The first concerns a passage about Christ's Ascension, which the Puritans believed supported the view that the souls of pre-Christian believers remained till then in the "Lake of the Fathers," a conception dangerous in that it might intimate belief in purgatory. Hooker denies that the passage suggests any dangerous interpretation. The Puritans objected to prayer against sudden death on the grounds that a Christian should be prepared to face death at any time. Hooker points out that sudden death in the Bible is often associated with evil or impiety, whereas the virtuous and pious die peacefully. The third passage is that in which believers pray that God grant them things which they in their unworthiness dare not ask for, wording which the Puritans found too servile. Hooker replies that the wording indicates both humility and faith. Another objection concerns the prayer in which the faithful ask to be delivered from all adversity, which the Puritans oppose on the grounds that the Bible makes no promise of this kind to man. Hooker cites Christ's prayer in the Garden as a precedent for this type of prayer and makes a long analysis of it. He also cites several other similar passages. The final objection, one fraught with doctrinal difficulty, is the prayer that all men may find mercy, which would seem to threaten belief in predestination. Hooker answers that the prayer reflects charity and confirms God's desire that all men be saved. Though to ask that all men be saved is to ask the impossible, the prayer does not run counter to the general will of God that all men be saved, only to his "more private *occasioned will* which determineth the contrarie" (5.49.3).

The Sacraments

Turning from instruction and prayer to the sacraments, Hooker examines the role of the church in perpetuating rites concerned in some manner with grace rather than with instruction. Thus he has very complicated theological problems to discuss, for the examination of sacraments leads him into an analysis of grace. About sacraments as ceremonies, he acknowledges that they include "two thinges, the substance of the ceremonie it selfe which is visible, and besides that somewhat els more secret in reference whereunto wee conceive that ceremonie to be a sacrament" (5.50.2) while he admits "still theire efficacie resteth obscure to our understandinge" (5.50.3). Sacraments are used only on earth, and they concern the afterlife; thus they are of utmost importance to man:

Sacramentes are the powerfull instrumentes of God to eternall life. For as our naturall life consisteth in the union of the bodie with the soule; so our life supernaturall in the union of the soule with God. And for as much as there is no union of God with man without that meane betwene both which is both, it seemeth requisite that wee first consider how God is in Christ, then how Christ is in us, and how the sacramentes doe serve to make us pertakers of Christ. (5.50.3)

This passage leads Hooker into the most profound theological analysis of *Ecclesiastical Polity* thus far—into the Trinity, the Incarnation, and Redemption. His view of the doctrines would be termed orthodox Christian for his time; he is at pains to give his understanding of the mysteries of faith, not interpreting them fully or saying anything new concerning them. Here as elsewhere he reviews ancient heresies concerning the Trinity and the Incarnation and explains the role of councils in settling them, particularly the Arian and Nestorian heresies. He dwells at length upon the image of Christ as both divine and human, retaining within one being both natures. This view makes for a complicated Christology, but Hooker emphasizes both natures. He formulates a kind of rule of Christ's nature: "of both natures there is a *cooperation* often, an *association* always, but never any mutuall *participation* whereby the properties of the one are infused into the other" (5.53.3). To explain more fully Christ as a source of grace for man, Hooker thus outlines the meaning of his two natures: "Christ is by three degrees a receyver, first in that he is the Sonne of God; secondlie in that his humane nature hath had the honor of

union with deitie bestowed upon it; thirdlie in that by meanes thereof
sundrie eminent graces have flowed as effectes from deitie in to that
nature which is coupled with it" (5.54.1). This union of God and
man has not changed in any way the divine nature but has changed
human nature by augmenting its potential perfection and by making
human beings associates of Deity, though it did not alter man's
nature beyond "those limites which our substance is bordered withall"
(5.54.5).

Hooker next turns to the question of Christ's presence, which he
considers essential for men to be "partakers of Christ." Unlimited
substance being in the nature of Deity, Christ may be said to be
omnipresent in his divine nature but not in his human. Augustine had
argued that Christ's ascension did not transform the human nature
of Christ, and therefore it continues to exist, even in heaven. Hooker
turns this argument neatly around. Since the divine and human
natures are inseparable, the human nature is in some sense involved
in the exercise of the divine. Like man, Christ has a human soul,
with powers of understanding and will, yielding in his full understanding of and assent to the divine will. Even the body of Christ
admits "in some sorte a kinde of infinite and unlimited presence," for
it too is joined in "a presence of true conjunction with deitie"
(5.55.9).

In explaining how Christ participates in the church and vice
versa, Hooker develops a chain of deductive arguments based upon
the Trinity as cause, leading to the general conclusion: "all thinges
which God hath made are in that respect the ofspringe of God, they
are *in him* as effectes in theire highest cause, he likewise actuallie is
in them, thassistance and influence of his deitie is *theire life*" (5.56.5).
Throughout all creation, though, only man experiences "savinge
efficacie" promised to men as sons of God. Hooker attaches weight to
the view that Christ is a second Adam, the spiritual father of mankind, all men being "spirituallie sithence descended and sproonge
out of him" (5.56.6). Now through a set of similes and metaphors,
which depict faith as a mystery, but which look like reasoning,
Hooker proceeds:

They which thus were in God eternallie by theire intended admission to
life, have by vocation or adoption God actuallie now in them, as the
artificer is in the worke which his hand doth presentlie frame.... But in
God wee actuallie are no longer then onlie from the time of our actuall

adoption into the bodie of his true Church, into the fellowship of his children. (5.56.7)

Relying on New Testament metaphors, Hooker presents the church as united with Christ as its head in a mystical conjunction through which man participates in Christ's nature: "except wee be trulie partakers of Christ, and as reallie possessed of his Spirit, all wee speake of eternall life is but a dreame" (5.56.7). He concludes that man gains immortality and incorruption, not so much through Christ's sacrifice (the Puritans would have stressed "Christ crucified") but rather through "the union of his deitie with our nature" (5.56.8), though sacrifice is important. But it is not Christ's spirit alone that sustains man. "Our corruptible bodies could never live the life they shall live, were it not that heere they are joyned with his body which is incorruptible..." (5.56.9). While the power and influence of Christ affect men in varying degrees, Christ is united fully and wholly, in his entire nature, in a mystical union with the church. For individual Christians, this union means "grace": "But the participation of Christ importeth, besides the presence of Christes person, and besides the mysticall copulation thereof with the partes and members of his whole Church, a true actuall influence of grace whereby the life which wee live accordinge to godlines is his, and from him wee receave those perfections wherein our eternall happines consisteth" (5.56.10). Man benefits from Christ's nature by imputation (benefits derived from Christ's death) and "by habituall and reall infusion, as when grace is inwardlie bestowed while wee are on earth..." (5.56.11).

This inward bestowal of grace to Christians on earth Hooker associates with the sacraments, they being more than ceremonies which teach. Hooker realizes that the theology of sacraments is complex, and he weighs a wide range of opinions about them before selecting the one he will develop and defend: "But theire chiefest force and virtue consisteth not herein so much as in that they are heavenlie ceremonies, which God hath sanctified and ordeined to be administred in his Church, first as markes wherebie to knowe when God doth imparte the vitall or savinge grace of Christ unto all that are capable thereof, and secondlie as meanes conditionall which God requireth in them unto whome he imparteth grace" (5.57.3). The grace comes from God, not from the rite itself, which is a mark or sign of God's grace, God desiring "to communicate by sensible meanes those bless-

inges which are incomprehensible" (5.57.3). Grace being a consequence, the sacraments are necessary and must be administered as
God directs.

Having clarified sacraments as fully as he can, Hooker turns to
the two recognized by the Church of England—Baptism and the
Eucharist. In their outward, tangible sense, sacraments require spoken
words and actions, though the church at its discretion may add
prayers and ceremonies. In case of emergency, a lay person is qualified to baptize. Through a figurative reading of the Bible, Cartwright
had minimized the necessity of Baptism for salvation and rejected
Baptism by laymen. Hooker cites the importance of literal interpretation and points to the unanimity of the historical church on this
point: "I holde it for a most infallible rule in expositions of sacred
scripture, that where a litterall construction will stand, the farthest
from the letter is commonlie the worst" (5.59.2). Through this
sacrament one enters the church and becomes a recipient of the
grace within it. Hooker compares the Puritans to the Valentinian
heretics of old who stressed knowledge over the sacraments, as the
Puritans stress faith.

Though the admonition of Christ about Baptism is unambiguous,
a kind of equity applies in interpreting Scripture. The verse from
John, "*Whoso beleiveth not the gospell of Christ is condemned
alreadie*" (5.60.5), does not apply to infants, deaf men, and the
mentally retarded. Some can gain salvation without the sacrament
as when a Christian suffers martyrdom before the sacrament can be
given; in such instances, a desire for Baptism is deemed sufficient.
As for infants who die unbaptized, Hooker defends the view that the
parents' interest or desire suffices: "God almercifull to such as are
not in them selves able to desire baptisme imputeth the secret desire
that others have in theire behalfe..." (5.60.6). But under normal
circumstances, Baptism is necessary, and though the church sets neither
time nor place for the rite, it is efficacious to infants—they being
capable of the grace it brings—and ought to be given.

Hooker then reviews positive laws concerning Baptism, regulating
time and place, and shows how these laws have altered, according to
prevailing conditions of the time, stressing the widely received view,
"*Baptisme by any man in case of necessitie*" (5.61.3), which he believes prevailed in the ancient church. Cartwright, in arguing against
infant Baptism and private Baptism under any circumstances, had
required that the ceremony be performed in church before the con-

gregation. Such limitations Hooker denounces, as "they savor not of Christ nor of his most gratious and meeke spirit, but under coulor of exact obedience they nourish crueltie and hardnes of harte" (5.61.5).

He refutes at length Cartwright's charge that Baptism by women is no more valid than an ordinary bath. There exists, Hooker argues, no scriptural prohibition of this practice, for administering the sacraments is not teaching. He surveys the history of the Church on the matter to show that neither heresy nor moral defect in the minister was considered a cause of an invalid Baptism and argues that the only justification for a second Baptism was a formal error in the first. He particularly attacks the Anabaptists for their insistence on rebaptizing converts.

When infants are baptized, promises of belief in and adherence to Christianity are expressed; to emphasize these at the ceremony the church directs questions or interrogatories to the person baptized, according to the Prayer Book. This positive, prescribed law the moderate Puritans who accept infant baptism oppose because an infant cannot understand the questions, much less answer them. Hooker defends the ceremony on the precedent from antiquity, on developmental grounds (the promises somehow help assure that the infant will develop in the right way), and on grounds of charity. He regards the ceremony as a kind of covenant in which for infants the promises to God are made by others, not necessarily by their parents. Hooker accepts the view that all infants, under any conditions whatever, may be baptized into the church and be bound by the promises made for them.

He answers at length the Puritan charge that marking the sign of the cross on the infant's head at Baptism is nonscriptural and reminiscent of popery, and therefore to be abhorred. He cites ancient precedent to defend its antiquity, to explain its symbolic significance, and to clarify its possible efficacy. He regards the use of this sign as a ceremony, making clear that he believes the Catholic use excessive.

To Hooker as well as to the Church of England, confirmation was an ancient ceremony of the church, involving the laying on of hands at an indefinite time following Baptism, not in itself a sacrament as held by Roman Catholics but a "sacrementall complement" (5.66.6). The patristic writers viewed the ceremony as one which strengthened Christian virtue and made a person more able to withstand temptation. Hooker believes that historically both Baptism and confirmation were performed during a single ceremony, and he points out that confirmation became the special province of bishops. At the end of this section Hooker lists the Puritans' arguments against confirmation and asserts that his general points are sufficient to answer them.

Hooker's treatment of the second sacrament of the church, "the Body and Blood of Christ," illustrates in a different manner his moderation. Frequently in *Ecclesiastical Polity* he seeks to defend a middle position by depicting the Puritans as extreme in one direction and Catholics in another. A less usual method or approach is to explore certain extremes of doctrine—in this instance Catholic "transubstantiation" and Lutheran "consubstantiation"—and then draw back without taking a definite stand, on the grounds that a definitive answer is unnecessary.

He regards the Eucharist as a necessary rite to sustain a Christian, because it provides grace against temptation. Exactly how grace is conveyed Hooker will not determine, except to argue that there is "the *reall participation of* Christe and of life in his bodie and bloode *by meanes of this sacrament*" (5.67.2). It must be remembered that to him a sacrament is a "sign" or "work," whose operation is in part mystical, and from the mystery he is willing to remain apart: "shall I wishe that men would more give them selves to meditate with silence what wee have by the sacrament, and lesse to dispute of the manner how? If anie man suppose that this were too greate stupiditie and dulnesse, let us see whether thappostles of oure lord them selves have not don the like" (5.67.3). If the Bible does not clarify the beliefs, neither do the early church fathers, who see it as a mystery. Citing the endless disputes that have arisen on this point, he is content to discourage speculation, on the basis of examples from the New Testament, a view consistent with his position that the essential points of faith are sufficiently clear in the Bible.

In an effort to clarify the matter as fully as possible, Hooker explores partly through logic, partly through metaphor, the workings of the Eucharist. It is clear from his discussion that grace does not come from a miraculous transformation of the bread and wine, no more than does the grace of Baptism come from the element of water:

The bread and cup are his bodie and blood because they are causes instrumentall upon the receipt whereof the *participation* of his bodie and bloode ensueth. For that which produceth any certaine effect is not vainely nor improperlie said to be that verie effect whereunto it tendeth. Everie cause is in the effect which groweth from it. Our soules and boodies quickned to eternall life are effectes the cause whereof is the person of Christ, his bodie and his bloode are the true wellspringe out of which this life floweth. (5.67.5)

The sacrament promotes a mystical union with Christ, the result being "The reall presence of Christes most blessed bodie and bloode is not therefore to be sought for in the sacrament, but in the worthie receiver of the sacrament" (5.67.6). His final statement of what Christ meant by the institution of the Eucharist is written as a re-interpretation of the words of Christ, and Hooker believes that all Christians can accept it, as far as it goes:

This hallowed foode, through concurrence of divine power, is in veritie and truth, unto faithfull receivers, instrumentallie a cause of that mysticall participation, whereby as I make my selfe whollie theires, so I give them in hande an actuall possession of all such saving grace as my sacri-ficed bodie can yeeld, and as theire soules do presently need, this is 'to them and in them' my bodie . . . (5.67.12)

Having stated a position which he believes all Christians can accept, he turns to answer objections about the manner of the church in administering the sacrament. He outlines six points which the Puritans had raised in objection, all of them minor, and most concerned with resemblance to the ceremony as given in Catholic churches. Hooker answers each objection in detail, spending the largest effort on that against administering communion to known Catholics. The Puritans had objected to speaking to every person as the sacrament is given, because it is nonscriptural. Hooker argues in justification that this practice fits the purpose of the sacrament and has a practical purpose as well. He defends other practices such as kneeling at communion and self-examination rather than examination by the minister beforehand, as appropriate acts of piety, the second having strong biblical precedent. Hooker defends the last two controversial practices—administering the sacrament to only a small portion of the congregation and giving private communion to the sick—as sound, not opposed to Scripture, and based upon well-established tradition.

Other Rites and Observances

Having considered the sacraments from both theological and ceremonial perspectives, Hooker next defends other ceremonies of the church. In his justification of festival days he begins with a general discussion of time, showing that man's awareness of it stems from celestial motion. Just as certain places, through extraordinary manifestation of God's presence, may be considered holy, so may times or days that indicate some extraordinary work of God. On these days it is fitting for the church to hold special services of thanksgiving, creating a solemnity consisting of promise, bounty, and rest. Hooker names the feast days of the church and argues ancient precedent and law: "the verie law of nature it selfe which all men confesse to be Godes law requireth in generall no lesse the sanctification of times then of places persons and thinges unto Godes honor" (5.70.9).

The Puritans objected that such holidays promote superstition and prayers for the dead, and Cartwright went so far as to condemn the celebration of Easter. Hooker views the feasts as having a kind of teaching function, to remind Christians of great religious truths and events. The Puritans had also issued a jurisdictional challenge, denying the church authority to establish religious holidays on the grounds that there were no specific scriptural commands for them. Hooker points out how a rationale of this kind would destroy all authority and applies his principle of positive law: "Those thinges which the Law of God leaveth arbitrarie and at libertie are all subject unto possitive lawes of men, which lawes for the common benefit abridg particular mens libertie in such thinges as farre as the rules of equitie will suffer. This wee must either mainteine or els overturne the world and make everie man his own commaunder" (5.71.4). He admonishes the Puritans to follow the law of the church rather than their own individual opinions and to regard the holidays as wholesome to the faith of believers.

As with feasts, so with fasting; Hooker defends the practice, both voluntary and mandatory, as beneficial to believers, grounded upon ancient precedent, including that of Christ himself, and sound according to the law of nature. Quoting Christ's admonition about fasting (Matthew 6:16), Hooker concludes, "Our Lord and Savior would not teach the maner of doing, much lesse propose a rewarde for doinge that, which were not both holie and acceptable in Gods sight" (5.72.4), and he discusses the customs and conventions of fasting among Jews and Christians. He defends the ordinances of fasting as reasonable and appropriate laws of the church. Historically fasting has been subject to abuses and excesses, particularly by heretics. But,

Hooker asserts, it has been rightly associated with penitence, both public and private, and has been perceived as a spur toward discipline and a guard against dissoluteness, thus beneficial to both the individual and society.

The concluding portions of the section on ordinances and ceremonies other than the sacraments include a defense of matrimony, churching of women after childbearing, and the burial service. Hooker explains marriage as necessary to the bearing and nurturing of children, and considers it a relationship founded upon "subalternation" (i.e., subordination) and inequality: "woman therefore was even in hir first estat framed by nature not onlie after in time but inferior in excellencie also unto man, howbeit in so due and sweet proportion as being presented before our eyes might be sooner perceyved then defind. And even herein doth lie the reason why that kind of love which is the perfectest ground of wedlock is seldome able to yeeld anie reason of it selfe" (5.73.2). The mysterious bond has a natural necessity, the offspring of man being slower to develop than those "of any other creature besides," and the required permanence of the bond makes it religious and scared. The rites of matrimony are traced to the Hebrews, who likewise considered them sacred.

The examination of marriage illustrates well Hooker's inclination to lay down general principles and justifications first, then deal with objections. In this instance the objections seem to have little to do with the principles, and his efforts may have been designed to achieve and clarify a common area of agreement before taking up areas of controversy. The Puritans objected, for example, to the church's prohibitions of the marriage ceremony during times designated for penance. Hooker answers Puritan objections to the use of the ring and the wording of the ceremony and the sacrament of the Eucharist by explaining their symbolism and significance.

The churching of women after childbirth was regarded not as a rite through which "purification in the old law did save" but as a time of thanksgiving for deliverance from a peril to women through original sin. In Hooker's view, the Puritan objection that it is still Jewish misses the mark and is merely wrongheaded; the objection to the woman's attire for the ceremony (veiled in white) is frivolous. The Puritan objection to the burial service seems to center upon the funeral sermon and prayers. Hooker sees the service as appropriately honoring the dead, grounded in Jewish practice, and a testimony of faith: "the greatest thing of all other about this dutie of Christian buriall is an outward testification of the hope which wee have touchinge the resurrection of the dead" (5.75.4).

The Ministry

The final section of book 5 concerns the public ministry of the Church. If religion represents the chief source of virtue in a civil state, it follows that "the Priest is a pillar of that commonwelth wherein he faithfullie serveth God" (5.76.1). His reading of history leads Hooker to the belief that a religious spirit provides some strength and security to the state, especially if the ruler is devout. He assumes that to have any beneficial effect in the state, religion requires a spiritual ministry—a proposition that he regards as self-evident.

A ministry implies organization, and organization to Hooker implies subordination or a hierarchy. He draws an analogy to nature, in a passage which illustrates how important the principle of subordination is to Hooker:

I could easilie declare how all thinges which are of God he hath by wonderfull arte and wisdome sodered as it were together with the glue of mutuall assistance, appointing the lowest to receive from the neerest to them selves what the influence of the highest yeeldeth. And therefore the Church beinge the most absolute of all his workes was in reason to be also ordered with like harmonie, that what hee worketh might no lesse in grace then in nature be effected by handes and instrumentes dulie subordinated unto the power of his own spirit. (5.76.9)

The metaphoric "harmonie" of the church polity reflects thus the hierarchy of nature, and Hooker, if pressed, would probably add of the choirs of angels. The rank or scale of being is self-evident, requiring no special justification.

Ministers enter the service of God through the rite of ordination, which derives from New Testament authority and which stamps recipients irrevocably; although they uphold the virtue of the state, they are not answerable to the state. "Ministeriall power is a marke of separation, because it severeth them that have it from other men and maketh them a speciall *order* consecrated unto the service of the most high in thinges wherewith others may not meddle" (5.77.2).

In the ordination service, the Puritans objected to the words to the new priest, "*Receive the holie Ghost,*" as either inappropriate or blasphemous, derived as they were from the New Testament (John 20:22). Hooker explains that the wording refers to the special work of the ministry and the powers needed for the work, that it does not signify the Holy Ghost but the gifts derived from God. Another objection is that the ministers indulge in ambition when they seek out a bishop to ordain them and produce letters of reference. As with other Puritan objections, this one seems an indirect attack on the bishops, but Hooker examines its professed intent and refutes it on rational grounds. As in other places he relies on definition, "Ambition as wee understand it hath bene accompted a vice which seeketh after honors inordinatlie" (5.77.10). After giving the definition, he has only to show that the ministers' requests are not inordinate.

A more serious problem is the Puritan attack upon degrees or orders within the church—their insistence that ministers be considered equals and their opposition to titles, such as "priest." Travers, for example, had signed himself "minister of the Gospel." Hooker finds precedent for hierarchy in the establishment and organization of the priestly tribe among the Jews. The need for hierarchy arose when priests become numerous and performed numerous duties. Hooker suggests that in the Christian clergy, "presbyter" and "deacon" should be the names of the two basic ranks and that he would gladly give up the title of "priest" to avoid needless offense toward the Puritans. Their main objection was that "priest" implies sacrifice rather than preaching the Gospel as the minister's primary duty.

Hooker divides the presbyters ordained by Christ into two orders, depending upon the powers of each—the Apostles being the smaller, more powerful order and other presbyters making up a second, larger one. So rapid was the growth of the church that deacons were established as stewards and as assistants to the presbyters during services, and the basic orders of the primitive church became apostles, presbyters, and deacons. Hooker approves of giving deacons additional duties (such as preaching) on the grounds that they are in fact clergymen and that an expansion of work in the church clearly justifies alterations in duties. He explains that the three ranks within the church were recognized in New Testament times and by the early church fathers. Other titles opposed by Puritans—dean, curate, vicar—are indicative of the kind of appointment a clergyman holds, not of his rank or degree.

Since a ministry requires material support, Hooker strongly urges the obligation that men contribute to the church. He views permanent donations, those that produce revenues or support in perpetuity, as superior to spontaneous charitable giving out of one's resources. Permanent gifts include temples and their ornaments and such bequests as land. Hooker surveys the practices of the Jews, finding precedent as usual from the Old Testament for some practices in the church, including tithing and donating land. Some analogies and correspondences at times strike one as farfetched, as when he justifies tithing on the grounds that the number ten represents nature's perfection, since all numbers above it repeat earlier ones. Tithes are derived from current incomes, and are the most appropriate kind of support, though man is no longer bound by the law that established them. Grants and gifts in perpetuity become the rightful property of the church, not to be taken away by civil authority. Hooker directs some of his strongest reproofs against those who are eager to seize upon church properties, but even here he shows his moderation: "I will not absolutelie saie concerninge the goodes of the Church that they maie in no case be seised on by men, or that no obligation commerce and bargaine made betwene man and man can ever be of force to alienate the propertie which God hath in them" (5.79.16). He regards the Puritan sympathy for and encouragement of man's covetousness in taking from the church as monstrously perverse and as derived from the church's "mortall enimie" (5.79.17).

Turning to the rights and duties of the ministry, Hooker points out that the ancient church, as a practical matter, was divided into precincts or parishes. These, however, were not independent congregations who elected their own presbyters or ministers. Had the ministerial appointment been local, Hooker asks, how could any minister in the line of duty have preached and converted pagans or infidels? Furthermore, leaving the power of selection to the local parish would in England overturn the system whereby ministers were first educated at the two universities for their particular vocation, ordained, and then appointed to parishes. "Presbyters and Deacons are not by ordination consecrated unto places but unto functions" (5.80.6). The places are varied, owing partly to history, partly to circumstances, partly to the number of clergy available. A landowner whose revenues support the parish church may have a voice in determining who the minister shall be.

Hooker now turns to three major Puritan objections: the clergy should be learned, they ought to reside in their parishes (against nonresidence), and they ought not to hold more than one spiritual

living each (against plurality). He concedes that the duties of a
minister and the solemn obligations of his office require learning.
He argues also for necessity of residence in the parish and argues
against plurality. But he disagrees with the Puritans by permitting dispensations under special circumstances (applying his fourth axiom),
and he proceeds to explain and defend dispensations as exceptions
necessary to achieve equity. Though the church is obligated to provide learned ministers, the two universities do not have the capacity
to produce all necessary replacements in a clergy that numbers twelve
thousand. Furthermore, not one fourth of the parishes have livings
sufficient for a learned man. In these circumstances, the church is
faced with two choices—to leave the positions unfilled or to ordain
men with "knowledg in that degree which is but tolerable" (5.81.5).
Since the Bible does not prescribe precisely how much knowledge a
minister must have, the church does not violate the law of God by
appointing ministers with less learning than it would wish. The Puritans ignore the dilemma faced by the church and condemn the apparent faults without pointing out to the people the worse alternative
of having no minister to perform the service and provide the sacraments.

The law which permits nonresidence also has a justifiable purpose
and effect: "The law giveth libertie of non residence for a time to
such as will live in universities, if they faithfullie there labor to grow
in knowledg that so they maie afterwardes the more edifie and the
better instruct theire congregations" (5.81.6). Further, clergymen may
be attached to the houses of noblemen and to courts, so that religion
will have a stronger influence upon rulers. Plurality too represents
a kind of exception whereby the church can adequately award exceptional service, merit, or responsibility. While dispensations may lead
to abuses, the church has within it the means to correct the abuses,
and Hooker at the close admonishes authorities to assure that the
dispensations do promote equity.

Conclusion

In book 5, Hooker has defended all the major ceremonies, rites, and
ordinances of the church: church buildings, preaching, the prayer
service, the sacraments, other rites and observances, and the ministry.
He has argued not that the way of the Church of England is the only
possible or permissible way, but rather that it is a reasonable way.

He examines and rejects the Puritan positions because they (1) do not assure improvement over present practice, (2) lack cogent rational or biblical foundation, or (3) are merely frivolous and wrongheaded. It is as though he says to Puritan opponents: Here is what the church does, along with a reason. You may be able to improve upon it, but nothing in your current stand in fact does.

A general assessment of Hooker's debt to his predecessors in the controversy with the Puritans seems in order. For his doctrine of sacraments he largely follows Jewel in an effort to distinguish the English theology from that of Catholicism and Lutheranism on the one hand and, on the other, the view held by some Puritans that the sacraments are only "signs." Along with other reformed churches, the Church of England reduced the number of sacraments from seven to two, but it could not regard them as mere signs without undermining the ministry and the hierarchy. Hooker's greatest debt remains to Whitgift. Not only does he repeat countless arguments and details used previously by Whitgift on specific points of controversy; he also takes important general approaches and principles from Whitgift: the analogy between the contemporary national church and "the church of the Jews," the assumption that in matters of polity a church appropriately reflects the society in which it exists, and the assumptions concerning the degrees of clergymen. Hooker's primary achievements are the following: He imposed an overall organization on the details of the controversy that was most effective for his polemic purpose. By selecting the order of service as a guide to organization, he effectively upheld its legitimacy. He derived his lines of argument from axioms clearly stated at the outset. Finally, he placed the issues of controversy in expanded theological and historical contexts.

Chapter Five
Ecclesiastical Polity,
Books 6-8:
Issues of Power
and Authority

The final three books of *Ecclesiastical Polity* have long been subject to uncertainty, doubt, and tentative conclusions as to authorship. Although Hooker lists them in his outline in 1593 and his wording to the reader suggests that they are nearly complete, they were not published until long after his death.[1] Books 6 and 8 were first published in 1648 by Richard Bishop, who had obtained the publication rights from William Stansby, and book 7 finally appeared in John Gauden's edition of 1662.

Conjectures about the cause of the delay have been numerous and varied. Hooker may not have completed either the drafts or their revisions before his death, so that they may not have been ready for publication. The reception and sale of previous publications may have been such that Sandys, who owned the rights to the work, was unwilling to publish the remaining books.[2] The manuscripts may have been suppressed and publication delayed by the influence of someone in the government or in the church.[3] Whatever the explanation, one has to examine the final books with some skepticism since their publication was neither overseen nor approved by the author. Despite the opportunities for corruption or censorship of the manuscripts during their passage through many hands following Hooker's death, there appears to have been little tampering with the text, except perhaps for book 6, which remains something of a mystery.

Hooker's outline calls for the following contents of the final books: (1) rejection of lay elders as a part of church polity, (2) a defense of the office and authority of bishops, and (3) a defense of the monarch as head of the church. These subjects involve a basic shift from book 5, where he defends rites and ceremonies of the church in detail, to broader questions of authority in the church and the origins of that authority. Book 6, as presented, differs from the other two, since it is intended as a refutation of a key Puritan position regarding polity, whereas books 7 and 8 clarify and defend the existing church polity.

The concerns of these books are echoed in a letter Hooker received from his former pupil George Cranmer. Writing probably after publication of book 5, Cranmer reviews the situation in the church, traces the decline of Elizabethan Puritanism, and suggests how Hooker might proceed to the completion of his work.[4] The most essential points of the Puritans are, he says, "overthrow of episcopal, erection of presbyterial authority."[5] These two aims, Cranmer believes, unite all Puritans. Satisfying all other objections they express against the church would not cause them to abandon their basic goals. He charges that their complaints are tactical, insincere, and frivolous, and suggests to Hooker that they undermine the state as well. He recommends that Hooker direct his arguments toward the clergy, even to the more learned among them, and that he urge the necessity for Christian ministry to put obedience above contention. The letter, like Cranmer and Sandys' notes on book 6, indicates the lasting friendship and mutual helpfulness that existed between Hooker and his former pupils. At the conclusion of book 5, Hooker appended this brief note to the reader, "Have patience with me for a small time, and by the helpe of Almightie God I will pay the whole" (2:535). The passage and Cranmer's letter suggest that books 6–8 were undergoing at least major revisions and perhaps some composition during the period 1597–1600.

Book 6: Lay Elders

In the opening paragraph of book 6, Hooker speaks of a lessening in the controversy, which in fact did occur after 1593, and speaks of the remaining issues of "the weightiest and last remains of that cause, Jurisdiction, Dignity, Dominion Ecclesiastical" (3:2). A strong appeal of the discipline proposed by the Puritans is that it leaves substantial jurisdiction in the hands of laymen; Hooker's purpose in book 6 is to reject that viewpoint. Having already discussed in book 5 the ceremonial and ritual duties of the minister and having explained that the clergy exist as a class apart from laymen, Hooker reaffirms in this book that a church is a society empowered to make canons or laws for its own operation. He turns to examine what is appropriately meant by the power of the church in "spiritual jurisdiction." The chief end of this function is to help men understand their sins and repent; thus, jurisdiction in the church has primarily to do with penitence. Inner repentance is the province of the individual; outward expression of repentance is the function of the church. Associated with outward repentance, or the "Discipline of Repentance," are rules or laws through which men perform reparations for their sins.

Genuine repentance to Hooker involves the desire for self-denial, reparation, and reform "with present works of amendment" (3:11). The proper stages of repentance are contrition, confession, and "works of satisfaction" (3:11). All three of these conditions apply to the virtue of repentance within the individual, but confession and satisfaction belong also to the discipline of penance, invested in the church.

Since Christ granted his Apostles "regiment in general over God's Church" (3:12), the church has the power and authority to make laws and to enforce them through courts and consistories. In order to cure men of sin, the church in ancient times imposed "offices of open penitence," sanctioned by Christ's original grant of authority. In time public confession ceased and the church instituted private confession to a priest, which it declared a sacrament. Hooker rejects the sacramental view after lengthy analysis and argues that confessions should be to God. Then he summarizes the various kinds of confessions among the Jews, pointing out that for injuries to and trespasses against others, public confession was encouraged. Yet neither this nor the biblical example of confession to the Apostles requires confession of sins to a priest, nor was private confession considered necessary in the ancient church "for many hundred years after Christ..." (3:23). He cites a series of patristic writers who recommend public confession for serious sin, not to deny that private confession existed but to stress that it was not considered mandatory. Both forms included satisfaction or duties imposed by a clergyman before penance was complete.

The role of the minister in the early church has bearing upon Hooker's position with regard to the laity: "men thought it the safest way to disclose their secret faults, and to crave imposition of penance from them whom our Lord Jesus Christ hath left in his Church to be spiritual and ghostly physicians, the guides and pastors of redeemed souls, whose office doth not only consist in general persuasions unto amendment of life, but also in the private particular cure of diseased minds" (3:31). Private confession to a priest became the ordinary mode, first in the Greek church, then in the Latin, because men were reluctant to acknowledge their most serious sins in public, but the forms of penance, as Hooker shows, were afterward subject to numerous alterations. The Greek church abolished public confession, and then Nectarius abolished all confession.

Even though penance is not a sacrament, Hooker considers it a duty, "both lawful and behoveful for God's people" (3:47). He surveys some of the practices of reformed churches, emphasizing private confession among Lutherans, and then explains the practice of the Church of England—a general, public acknowledgment of sins, followed by absolution by the minister. Hooker believes this general form of confession is adequate, provided that the people are truly penitent. But just as some men take no heed of their sin, others weigh it too heavily and are troubled by scruples. For these the church permits private confession, the advice of the clergyman, and absolution, a form of confession especially applicable to those approaching death. The practice of the church, then, is to discourage public confession of specific sins, to include in the prayer service general confession and absolution, and to permit in special instances private confession and absolution.

Since justice logically requires a measure of reparation—particularly when a sinner's deed has harmed another person—Hooker considers satisfaction following confession, defined as follows: "The name of Satisfaction, as the ancient Fathers meant it, containeth whatsoever a penitent should do in the humbling himself unto God, and testifying by deeds of contrition the same which confession in words pretendeth" (3:55). Because no one may satisfy his sin against God, an infinite wrong which only Christ's sacrifice can satisfy, laws regarding satisfaction are designed to require little. Yet even private repentance, if sincere, requires some attention to satisfaction—prayers, fasts, and alms deeds being the usual means, though some sins require that satisfaction in the form of restitution be made to men harmed by the sins. The manner of restitution and reparation was at times defined in the ancient church by canon law, which commonly required denial of communion until satisfaction was made. Whereas the ancient church required satisfaction before absolution, the practice of the Roman church is to provide absolution first. Hooker agrees with the Roman view that a minister has the power to absolve sins but draws attention to the differences with Rome regarding penance. In the

Church of England, absolution by the priest is not considered essential to forgiveness.

Whereas Hooker does not deny that repentance by an individual can be adequate in God's sight, he accords ministers two important roles. The first concerns the fitness or propriety of church services regarding penance: "To remission of sins there are two things necessary; grace, as the only cause which taketh away iniquity; and repentance, as a duty or condition required in us. To make repentance *such as it should be*, what doth God demand but inward sincerity joined with fit and convenient offices for that purpose? the one referred wholly to our own consciences, the other best discerned by them whom God hath appointed judges in this court" (3:77; italics mine). The ministers, metaphorically judges, determine what a fit office is. They also are responsible for two kinds of penitents, those who repent voluntarily and those "such as are to be brought to amendment by ecclesiastical censure..." (3:78). In this second kind of spiritual jurisdiction, "which by censures constraineth men to amend their lives; it is true, that the minister of God doth more than declare and signify what God hath wrought" (3:79). Absolution presupposes sincere repentance on the part of the sinner and is not a one-way exercise of power, but censure for sin remains a clerical power.

Hooker follows with a reexamination of the Catholic view of penance as a sacrament, stoutly opposing the viewpoint, as well as the viewpoint of Aquinas and the pronouncement of the Council of Trent regarding the power of sacraments generally. In this he repeats material covered in book 5, and belabors an apparent contradiction in Catholic doctrine regarding penance as a sacrament.

At the end he returns to a theme raised earlier about inordinate guilt and anguish in those whose minds are troubled by a sense of sin, particularly those who believe they have committed the unpardonable sin. Hooker appears to regard the unpardonable sin as apostasy, for those who persist in it. Yet some "wrong themselves with over rigorous and extreme exactions..." (3:105), guilt driving them to perform excessive acts in the hope of satisfaction. It becomes the duty of the minister to reassure them about their souls, to explain that God does not require perfection but rather a sincere heart, sorrowful for sin.

As it stands, book 6 appears to be, as Keble said, about ninety-five percent digressive. Only a small portion of the work deals with the subject of lay elders. The manuscript repeats two paragraphs in differ-

ent spots, contains a large gap of perhaps half a page, and omits the
chapter titles at the beginning. Though Keble accepted the work as
authentic, he assumed that it was a fragment of some kind inserted
by an editor as the major section of book 6. It is possible that the
work represents a lost sermon on the subject of penance, or that
Hooker first intended it for inclusion in book 5, where he writes of
penance as another rite of the church. He may then have decided
against including in a book already very long an account only tan-
gential to his main purpose.

An additional reason for assuming that Hooker did not intend
book 6 as it now stands arises from a set of notes compiled by George
Cranmer and Edwin Sandys in response to a manuscript copy of
book 6, probably in 1597 or 1598. Cranmer's notes, the more extensive, appear first, followed by those of Sandys. Each provides page
numbers and catch words for the notes, which show that Hooker's
manuscript included at least eighty-five pages. The notes do not make
merely editorial corrections and comments; some are substantive, so
much so that Keble was able to assemble from the notes a conjectural
outline of the manuscript seen by Cranmer and Sandys (1:xxxvi).
Keble demonstrates beyond doubt that except for the first portion, the
text of book 6 in no way follows the outline of the manuscript
critiqued by Hooker's pupils. He concludes that the text has been
corrupted, perhaps by the Puritans, and that the major portions might
well be separated from *Ecclesiastical Polity.*

The notes of Cranmer and Sandys warrant extended discussion.
First, Hooker's pupils had previously seen a manuscript of book 7,
for Cranmer refers to it. Second, both thought Hooker's conclusion
weak and recommended strengthening it; Sandys thought Hooker
should enlarge the scope of the book. Third, their comments clearly
treat the manuscript as a rough draft susceptible to many alterations
and additions. The nature of their comments and advice becomes
evident in these words of Sandys, a member of Parliament, on cases
of "mixed" law—that is, any law that involves both civil and ecclesiastical matters: "The canon law I know greatly urgeth that all mixt
causes be ecclesiasticall, for honour of that part: which seemes hard
to yeald to, at least wise it would be now hardly taken to require it.
These thinges you must needes handle somewhere or other" (3:132).
It is clear that they offer candid criticism of difficult issues treated in
the manuscript, for instance, ecclesiastical courts.

The notes reveal that approximately one third of Hooker's manuscript dealt with the precedent derived from clerical or ministerial power among the Jews. Here both Cranmer and Sandys are thorough and severe in their criticism, suggesting that Hooker has either erred or reached conclusions that his sources do not warrant. In fact, Cranmer urges a kind of general caveat in which Hooker admits that the ancient history of the Jews is such that one cannot conclude very much with assurance but that "partly out of Scripture, partly by probable coniecture and out of the writinges of the Jewes you have collected and sett downe that which in your opinion is most consonant unto trueth" (3:118). He then summarizes Hooker's main argument about the Jews under thirteen points, which indicate an emphasis upon separation of religious and lay duties in the Jewish state. Further, Cranmer and Sandys suggest that Hooker clarify the position of his opponents—which he is supposedly refuting—and one gets the impression that he had little to say about it. This is an oddity, for in book 6 he is attempting to do what he did in book 2, to overturn or refute an important Puritan position. His approach in book 6 appears to resemble more that of book 5, where he makes the case for the Church of England on the precedent of pre-Christian Jews, the early church, or both, and then deals with Puritan arguments opposed to it.

Keble's inclination to reject the surviving text of book 6, which differs drastically from the manuscript reviewed by Sandys and Cranmer, may be mistaken. Faced with extensive and probing criticism, Hooker may have chosen to retreat from the more complicated issues that his approach had raised. Since he did not need to argue for the controversial rights of ecclesiastical courts or the power of excommunication, he may have found it prudent to restrict his inquiry. The long discourse on the Jews was perhaps too tentative and uncertain to establish or refute any position on the separation of clergy and laity. To reorient his account toward spiritual jurisdiction in connection with the minister's power over penance may have appeared a preferable approach, as Houk suggested.[6] To Hooker it was obvious that lay elders would render the ministerial roles of confessor and absolver extremely difficult, but he has not clarified that point in book 6 as it stands. It seems an inescapable conclusion that the book was incomplete at the time of Hooker's death. The suggestion by Houk that he may have contemplated another section entitled "Agents of Spiritual Jurisdiction—Lay Elders" appears plausible.[7]

Book 7: Bishops

Book 7, the last part of *Ecclesiastical Polity* to see publication, appeared in John Gauden's edition of 1662. Gauden, then bishop of Exeter, wrote a life of Hooker to accompany the edition, a biography so inaccurate that Gilbert Sheldon, archbishop of Canterbury, asked Izaak Walton to write a replacement. Despite the questionable actions of Gauden during the civil wars and his unreliable biography, the authenticity of book 7 has never been seriously challenged. Though no manuscript is known to be extant, Keble found the internal evidence of Hooker's authorship unassailable.[8]

The book attempts to answer the Puritan opposition to the bishops, a long-standing and important quarrel. So long as bishops remained, the church retained a hierarchy, and it appeared to Puritans that a Catholic monarch might easily restore the Roman church. Had not John Knox warned that the best way to keep the rooks from returning was to tear down their nests? And Thomas Cartwright had asserted that it was not adequate to dismount the pope, that one had to take away the stirrups so that he could not climb back into the saddle.

The twenty-four chapters of book 7 may be classified under three headings: chapters 1–2 explain the origin and history of the office of bishop; chapters 3–16 outline the bishops' authority and powers and review arguments against them; chapters 17–24 defend the honors and privileges of English bishops.

Origins and History. In the opening section Hooker uses an anecdotal account of a reformer who urged his audience that in order for a nation to bear good fruit, three great branches needed to be lopped off—nobles, lawyers, and prelates—showing that the result of this rash innovative spirit was confusion within the nation. Reformers in England have been content, he argues, to begin with prelates, but their intent goes far beyond their present effort, which has subjected bishops to mockery and abuse. In contrast to the spirit of innovation, Hooker places the example of the past, with all its force: "A thousand five hundred years and upward the Church of Christ hath now continued under the sacred regiment of bishops" (3:143). The imposing weight of historical evidence establishes the divine origin of a rank whose success in society remains unquestioned. He traces the existence of bishops in England from the second century (following Bede) and denounces as shallow the spirit of innovation that would alter it: "some wicked thing hath undoubtedly bewitched us, if we forsake that government, the use whereof universal experience hath for so many years approved, and betake ourselves unto a regiment neither appointed of God himself, as they who favour it pretend, nor till yesterday ever heard of among men" (3:144).

A part of the Puritan argument, he notes, had been to accept ancient bishops as legitimate and worthy and then to deny, on the basis of external and superficial differences, that modern bishops are their true successors. In response he examines the essential conditions common to early bishops and those of his own time. He explains that the Greek origins of "bishop" implied guide and overseer and explains how the term came to mean a principal ecclesiastical overseer.

Hooker argues that from the beginning of the church, bishops have had superiority, not only in the sense of exclusive duties, but also in the sense of power over other ministers. He examines the power of ancient bishops under four headings: its origin, its demonstrative evidence from antiquity, its manner of governance from ancient testimony, and its extent. The office originated with the Apostles who were messengers and teachers to the people, but were also bishops by virtue of their serving as governors of the early church. Hooker grants that the episcopal power they exercised may not have been limited to a definite area, as it was with later bishops, although in the instance of James, bishop of Jerusalem, it was. According to the New Testament and early fathers of the church, the Apostles handed down their authority to other bishops, who became the authorities for settling disputes within the church. Hooker cites St. Augustine for proof that by his time bishops were universally established and shows that a Puritan interpretation of a passage from St. Jerome, seeming to indicate that bishops were established only in Alexandria, is incorrect.

It is in this section that Hooker deals with the question of apostolic succession. Bishops could argue, as some did, that they were the true descendants of the Apostles in a sacred office instituted by Christ. Hooker denies that the power of the bishop actually stems from divine command. He admits that the Apostles did appoint bishops and were bishops and that the appointment was "not without the special direction of the Holy Ghost" (3:164); on the other hand, the institution of bishops was a positive law of the Apostles, subject to repeal if the church saw fit: "On the other side bishops, albeit they may avouch with conformity of truth that their authority hath thus descended even from the very apostles themselves, yet the absolute and everlasting continuance of it they cannot say that any commandment of the Lord doth enjoin; and therefore must acknowledge that the Church hath power by universal consent upon urgent cause to take it away..." (3:165). On the question of apostolic succession, he thus identifies himself as a moderate, willing to uphold tradition, yet recognizing that the law supporting the tradition rests upon reason. As with kings, so with bishops: a legitimate polity may exist without them, since Christ's divine ordination of the Apostles was of individuals, not of an office. But lest he be thought to concede too much, he turns to Jerome's other argument that bishops were created through the instigation of the Holy Ghost: "if any thing in the Church's government, surely the first institution of bishops was from heaven, was even of God, the Holy Ghost was the author of it" (3:168). This is indeed strong ground for believing the office necessary and beneficial, but not adequate for any single bishop or group of bishops to see themselves as indispensable.

Powers and Authority.   Bishops hold the special and exclusive rights of ordaining ministers and of exercising ecclesiastical jurisdiction—moderating disputes, appointing special ceremonies and fasts, and disciplining ministers. Hooker cites Jerome, Cyprian, and Chrysostom to confirm the distribution of power and responsibilities between bishops and presbyters. He likewise illustrates from the testimony of early fathers that the power of bishops extended beyond one church or parish to the see or diocese. For as the organization of the church increased in scope and along with it the number of bishops, it became expedient to establish some bishops over others as presiding officers. Bishops of metropolitan cities within the Roman Empire became archbishops, and later some archbishops of major metropolitan centers became primates, until the primate of Rome in time became the pope. The primate's chief function was apparently to assist the bishops in quelling heresy, so that ample precedent exists for the office of archbishop.

Having demonstrated the differing degrees or ranks in early Christianity, Hooker turns to the Puritan arguments that such differences are a modern innovation not supported by Scripture. He undertakes an analysis, pointing out that the biblical passages are somewhat ambiguous, but that even in the absence of strong biblical support, the office of bishop is not therefore compromised. He returns to apply his principle regarding the law of nature: "The law of nature then being his law, that must needs be of him which it hath directed men unto" (3:213). Thus the bishops as an institution can stand, even without belief in apostolic succession.

Hooker proceeds to answer opposition on particular points, urging that the Puritan reading of the early history of the church regarding bishops is fallacious. To the argument that bishops are unnecessary because the judicial authority can be exercised at the congregational level, Hooker responds by making an analogy to the state, showing the need for courts of appeal: "which hath been always observed every where in civil states, and is no less requisite also for the state of the Church of God" (3:220–21). To answer the objections that the bishops exercise power beyond that of their predecessors, he argues that bishops have acquired their powers in the body politic of the church through the orderly development of laws. For example, the role of bishops in ordaining ministers more nearly resembles the New Testament ordination by the Apostles than the selection of ministers by the congregation, as the Puritans advocate. He particularly objects to congregational power of selecting ministers because the ministry of a clergyman is not limited to a congregation. He shows that ancient practice of the church was ordination by bishops, though he admits as exceptions direct authorization from God or ordination when a bishop cannot function. In the system whereby bishops and landowners select pastors, the people have a choice only indirectly, "yet can they not say that they have their pastors violently obtruded upon them, inasmuch as their ancient and original interest therein hath been by orderly means derived into the patron who chooseth for them" (3:232).

Hooker briefly defends the civil power of bishops to order offenders jailed by arguing a precedent from the Jews and by pointing out that the justice in each individual sentence is what should determine the issue. For the bishops' participation in other civil affairs, Hooker examines man's ability to separate spiritual from civil or secular affairs and finds the distinction difficult to make. For example, the main function of universities is to produce clergymen; should these institutions of the nation be ruled totally by secular officers and laws? Should a nobleman, who happens to be a clergyman, be forced to give up his ministry if chance makes him a governor of a civil state? Hooker argues that a kind of economy exists in grace as well as in nature that should enable men to exercise their talents to the fullest. This principle implies that kings may make civil officers of church

officials. Those who consider this power a violation of divine law mis-
interpret the Scripture and the patristic writers. On the office of
the bishop and the powers that accompany it, he concludes: "In the
writings of the ancient Fathers, there is not any thing with more
serious asseveration inculcated, than that it is God which maketh
bishops, that their authority hath divine allowance, that the bishop
is the priest of God, that he is judge in Christ's stead, that according
to God's own law the whole Christian fraternity standeth bound to
obey him. Of this there was not in the Christian world of old any
doubt or controversy made, it was a thing universally every where
agreed upon" (3:261). Again he points to the universal assent of
mankind as the voice of God itself and the unanimous testimony of
the ancient fathers as a matter of weight. Those who will not accept
such guides exalt private judgment so high as to deny legitimacy to
all superiors.

Honors and Privileges. On the more difficult question of the
honors appropriate to bishops, Hooker explains that degree in life
naturally admits of degree in honor. Outward signs of honor—titles
and insignia of office—are only superficial indicators of where honor
should be directed. He believes that honor due to bishops is not
merely traditional but effects a public good, because without them
the exercise of true religion in the state "cannot well and long continue" (3:264). The example of Aaron demonstrates the benefit
to society of spiritual regiment, and "Bishops are now as high priests
were then, in regard of power over other priests..." (3:266). Historically, the church has benefited, beyond doubt, from the prelacy.
Through their role as superiors or overseers, the bishops have used
their authority to assure that the church carries on its work effectively.

Hooker classifies the public, external honors due to bishops as
those of title, place, ornament, attendance, privilege, and endowment
and argues in defense of all of them. Bishops appropriately have
forms of address, distinctions of rank, special attire ("ornaments"), a
variable number of attendants for honor as well as assistance. In
chapter 21 Hooker arrives at an issue that George Cranmer in his
letter had alluded to, one that had been important in church affairs
since the time of Henry VIII and especially during the reign of
Edward VI—the honoring of bishops with wealth. Hooker's rhetoric
on the matter is intense; he speaks of "the sacrilegious intention of
Church robbers, which lurketh under this plausible name of Reformation" (3:281–82). The schemes of those who sought to deprive

the church of wealth and properties had created major problems for Elizabeth's bishops—especially for the archbishops Matthew Parker, Edmund Grindal, and John Whitgift—who on occasion took courageous steps to preserve the holdings and rights of the church. The properties of the church are really God's, Hooker argues, returned to Him by men who first received them at His hands. God's ownership of property is founded upon many biblical passages of both Testaments which lead Hooker to the following conclusion: "God doth not refuse to be honoured at all where there lacketh wealth; but where abundance and store is, he there requireth the flower thereof, being bestowed on him, to be employed even unto the ornament of his service" (3:291). Scripture is also a precedent for the stewardship of God's properties being vested in His ministers, and ancient practice has placed this responsibility in the bishops' hands.

Distribution of income and revenue in the Jewish religion recognized rank and privilege. The bishops' power over disposition of revenues naturally led to questions and to opposition, and some abuses from earlier times had been corrected. As one remedy, a fixed ample amount (one fourth of the diocesan revenues) was set aside to each bishop's use, yet some considered this amount excessive. Hooker responded that these revenues belong to the church, not to the bishop who enjoys them, and to deprive the church of them is sacrilege.

In justifying the income of bishops as appropriate to their office and in arguing in support of preservation of church property, Hooker includes a passage in praise of Queen Elizabeth for her record on the question. Yet confiscation of monastic properties under Henry VIII was in part just, for the monks "were properly no portion of God's clergy (only such amongst them excepted as were also priests)" (3:321), so that their holdings could be compared with those of a corporation or city. Even so, the dissolution of these religious houses brought little good to society, only to individuals. If the wealth of the church was once excessive, the excesses have been removed, and no further confiscation of church properties should occur. Hooker believes that revenues amounting to 126,000 pounds yearly have already been removed from the church, enough to provide adequate livings for more than four thousand clergymen. He concludes with the pleas that the position of the clergy be maintained and that no further spoilation of the church occur.

Book 8: Royal Supremacy

The eighth book of *Ecclesiastical Polity*, first published with book 6 in 1648, answers the Puritan objection to the power of the king or monarch over the church, which in England had been established by the law in 1532 making the prince the temporal head of the church. Headings for the book's nine chapters were originally provided by James Ussher, archbishop of Armaugh, who had in his possession two manuscript copies. The reasons for accepting the authenticity of book 8 have been carefully outlined by Houk, and no serious question appears to remain.[9] Archbishop Ussher entitled the first three chapters "Of Kings and their Power Ecclesiastical Generally" and the remaining six "Of the Kings of England particularly," divisions which Houk believes consistent with those of books 6–7.[10]

Hooker begins his defense of "power of ecclesiastical dominion" vested in the prince by a reference to the ancient Jews, whose kings were also religious leaders. Jewish kings made laws in matters of "mere" religion—that is, unmixed with secular affairs: "According to the pattern of which example, the like power in causes ecclesiastical is by the laws of this realm annexed unto the crown" (3:328). Opponents of this arrangement raise two main arguments against it: that church and state should be separate and that the church should be governed by "Christian governors" from within. Hooker gives careful consideration to each of these.

A church is that body politic within a state which represents and maintains true religion, as did the religious polity of the ancient Jews. Hooker grants that church and commonwealth may be considered as separate entities or societies, but the nationalistic ideal of the Renaissance permits him to view them as closely complementary: "We hold, that seeing there is not any man of the Church of England but the same man is also a member of the commonwealth; nor any man a member of the commonwealth, which is not also of the Church of England; therefore . . . no person appertaining to the one can be denied to be also of the other" (3:330). Joint membership by all members of the societies permits the exercise of rights and powers in both. "For the truth is, that the Church and the commonwealth are names which import things really different; but those things are accidents, and such accidents as may and should always dwell lovingly together in one subject" (3:336). This is an example of Hooker's ideal of unity, perhaps in this instance somewhat removed from reality.

Hooker next examines the lawful exercise of power by the monarch—"what the power of dominion is"—along with church matters in which the king's dominion may be felt. Order in any society requires degrees, marked by relative amounts of power, dominion being the highest. The king's powers are limited by God's commands, by law, and by established power belonging to groups within a society. Hooker acknowledges that the king's dominion over the church is not commanded by Scripture but asserts that once established, it has the stamp of God's approval. Jesus ordered that tribute be paid to Tiberius, even though Tiberius was not appointed by God. "That the Christian world should be ordered by kingly regiment, the law of God doth not any where command; and yet the law of God doth give them right, which once are exalted to that estate, to exact at the hands of their subjects general obediences in whatsoever affairs their power may serve to command" (3:346). Once granted, dominion cannot be withdrawn without the consent of the ones to whom it is granted, though if there is none to inherit dominion the power may return to the body that granted it.

The scope of a king's power is determined by the original compact, by positive laws, and by tradition, as well as the laws of God and nature. Aristotle, as quoted by Hooker, seemed to believe that the best kings were the most restrained, but Hooker disagrees somewhat:

I am not of opinion that simply always in kings the most, but the best limited power is best: the most limited is, that which may deal in fewest things; the best, that which in dealing is tied unto the soundest, perfectest, and most indifferent rule; which rule is the law; I mean not only the law of nature and of God, but very national or municipal law consonant thereunto. Happier that people whose law is their king in the greatest things, than that whose king is himself their law. (3:352)

Hooker concludes that kings may lawfully exercise dominion over religion, that their dominion does not extend to the normal duties of clergymen—administering the sacraments, ordination, and ecclesiastical jurisdiction—and that the necessary rule of the king's actions over the church is not fully or clearly established in England. To clarify the need for rule, he cites limitations on the king's dominion in civil affairs and quotes Ambrose, " 'kings have dominion to exercise in ecclesiastical causes, but according to the laws of the Church' " (3:358).

In answering Puritan objections to royal supremacy, Hooker considers naming the king "head" of the church, the Puritans' point being that the title belongs only to Christ. At length Hooker shows that *head* applied to the king differs from the meaning applied to Christ. This section includes an interesting discussion of Christ as the Word, and as king, priest, prophet, and acknowledged spiritual head of the church. As temporal head of the church, the king has the power of calling church councils or synods, a right established by precedent of the Jews and the Christian emperors of Rome. But the king, who does not rule by right of conquest, cannot claim an absolute authority to make canon law: "nature itself doth abundantly authorize the Church to make laws and orders for her children that are within her" (3:396). Neither does the hierarchy enjoy the power of jurisdiction through divine right, "as ours also do imagine" (3:397).

He next examines the manner of establishing canon law through church council or convocation. The crux of the question is whether the prelates themselves in council, representing the clergy, have the power of passing laws, or whether their proposals must be approved by the king in order to become law. New laws being necessary from time to time, the power for instituting them for the church should be clear, whether they relate to doctrine or to polity. A difficult question involves laws relating to doctrine. Hooker asserts that laws do not really establish true belief, but only direct men away from false beliefs by pointing out the truth. Second, they are difficult to enforce: "as opinions do cleave to the understanding, and are in heart assented unto it is not in the power of any human law to command them, because to prescribe what men shall think belongeth only unto God" (3:401).

The authority of making laws for the church being derived from the entire society, it is not clear in what forum the authority must be exercised. Councils of clergymen cannot claim an absolute right on the analogy to the Council of Jerusalem, for no council since has had equal authority, and Hooker prefers to leave the matter somewhat ambiguous: "we are to hold it a thing most consonant with equity and reason, that no ecclesiastical law be made in a Christian commonwealth, without consent as well of the laity as of the clergy, but least of all without consent of the highest power" (3:404). To pass and impose canon laws without the consent or understanding of the laity seems somehow unjust: "Peace and justice are maintained by preserving unto every order their rights, and by keeping all estates as it were in an even balance" (3:405). Thus the canons of a general church council have no force of law without approval of the public (through Parliament) and the king. Hooker grants that Parliament, the broadest representative body, has the power of passing laws applicable to the Church. Parliament with the convocation "is that whereupon the very essence of all government within this kingdom doth depend; it is even the body of the whole realm . . ." (3:408). He points out the anomaly that could arise if the king had to enforce a law which he opposed. The voice of the king, on the precedent of early emperors, is most fittingly a veto over laws passed by the clergy or by clergy and laymen.

While bishops alone consecrate, the king "elects," that is, "selects" a bishop and appoints him to his diocese. The laws of Henry VIII made, in fact, the consecration and the concurrence by other bishops little more than an appendage of the royal will. This bishop not only becomes a spiritual nobleman but receives a position as one of the chief financial officers of the church. In both roles a Tudor monarch had a keen and, to Hooker, appropriate interest. "Election" thus fittingly precedes consecration. For this kind of power vested in the king, Hooker finds analogies with foreign governments and especially with the Roman Empire, citing the disputes between kings and popes during the Middle Ages over the appointment of bishops. While he approves of the king's prerogative, Hooker acknowledges that abuses can occur, as when kings do not select those most fit for the office, or leave sees vacant while enjoying their revenues, or tax the dioceses too heavily—practices that Tudor monarchs had permitted at one time or another.

In addition to the appointment of bishops, the king enjoys a wide range of powers over ecclesiastical services and teaching. He may also participate in councils and serve as a judicial officer. The king must approve directives and commands to the entire national church. Direct intervention into church matters by the monarch was unusual, but clearly a constitutional possibility. An extraordinary instance occurred in 1577 when Queen Elizabeth sent a royal directive to all bishops ordering the suppression of gatherings of ministers called "prophesyings," sermons before mixed audiences of clergy and lay-men. Hooker considers the royal power a kind of final court, to be employed on appeal or in exceptional circumstances.

His final defense of the Tudor settlement concerns the king's im-munity from censure by ecclesiastical courts. Hooker argues that the king, as the source of lawful authority, must of necessity be above that authority and therefore punishable by God only. Citing negative evidence from Scripture, he argues that no early king of the Jews was excommunicated. Against the precedent of the Emperor Theodosius's excommunication by St. Ambrose, and the emperor's submission, Hooker argues that it was an example of "extraordinary zeal on both sides, and not [a proceeding] from a settled judicial authority" (3:453), since Ambrose did not possess the authority to punish the emperor. Hooker agrees that a clergyman has the right to deny the sacraments to an evil or sinful king, yet the church possesses no settled judicial authority to pass sentence upon kings.

Chapter Six
The Legacy of Richard Hooker

Despite formidable disadvantages, Hooker's treatise has earned a place as a literary classic. His reputation rests solely upon *Of the Laws of Ecclesiastical Polity*, a work left incomplete at his death and published in installments over nearly seventy years. His synthesis remains impressive but is generally regarded as looking toward the past—the Middle Ages and early Christianity—rather than toward the future.

In marshaling and supporting his positions, Hooker draws from a multitude of sources and authorities—classical, biblical, judaic, patristic, and Renaissance. For the outward form of the early Christian church he relies heavily upon the early fathers Irenaeus, Chrysostom, and Hilary of Poitiers. Yet the most pervasive influence upon his thought concerning man and his institutions was Aristotle and the medieval Aristotelian, St. Thomas Aquinas. These influences are not easily distinguished, for it is difficult to ascertain whether a writer follows Aristotle directly or through other sources; one speaks of Neoplatonism but not of neo-Aristotelianism. For his views on entelechy, the nature of man, the primacy of reason, causation, moderation, and the nature of politic societies, Hooker remains firmly within the tradition of Aristotle. For such positions as the nature of man's soul, the final end of man, the existence of *lex aeterna*, the divine basis of all law, the significance of natural law, and the church as an institution, he reveals a debt to St. Thomas Aquinas. He differs from his predecessors in his broader understanding and application of terms like "law" and "church" and, more importantly, in using their ideas to defend the concept of an independent national church existing within the universal church, a position that would have been unpalatable to Aquinas.

Hooker wrote as the Elizabethan Age was drawing to its close, when the assumptions and values of both Puritanism and the Church of England were changing. Thus his ideas seemed often inapplicable or unacceptable during the seventeenth century. Though he founded no school, left no imitators, initiated no lasting intellectual contro-

versy, he did leave an imprint on English prose style and, in a be-
wildering number of ways, on the intellectual history of the nation.

Prose Style

Analyses of Hooker's style to date have been limited, though valuable, and much work remains to be done.[1] To early critics like Saints-
bury and Krapp, Hooker wrote an English prose remarkable for its
clarity, grace, and modernity—a style dignified, stately, rhythmic—a
fitting reflection of the man himself. Analyses of his style, usually
based upon the most familiar portions of *Ecclesiastical Polity*, led to
the accepted commonplace that Hooker stood out as a polemicist who
retained a dignified, elevated tone and respect for his opponents.
While the generalization contains both truth and justice, especially
in comparison with his contemporaries and successors in religious controversy, it is not entirely reliable. Hooker did resort at times to
irony and sarcasm, though not often against his Puritan opponents.
While he generally postulates a reasonable adversary, he can speak
in a range of tones, and the reader of Hooker's prose encounters a
number of personae. The majesterial teacher, the fellow Christian,
the offended cleric, the humble penitent, the wise expounder of
maxims, the respectful student of philosophers and church fathers,
the nationalist—all of these and more one encounters, though one
does not find the persona that John Bunyan so fittingly names
Evangelist.

To analyze Hooker's style is to focus upon his sentences and the
stylistic features that they embody. Since he recognizes that he is
writing a treatise, he marshals the ideas carefully. He divides his
subject logically and provides clear introductions and effective, sometimes eloquent, conclusions to the sections of his work. Yet the reader
of Hooker may encounter difficulty with his typically long and periodic
sentences. Though he does use numerous short sentences for variation and emphasis, those that Cicero called "little daggers," his usual
sentence is quite long. Georges Edelen finds that the sentences of
Ecclesiastical Polity, book 1, range from two words to two hundred
and sixty-seven and that slightly more than half exceed forty words.[2]
One sentence from the fifth book (5.76.8) exceeds five hundred
words. Hooker constructs his sentences through the use of subordinate
clauses, parentheses, appositives, and nominative absolutes, normally
exerting careful control over the complex structures which he erects.

One of Hooker's typical sentences illustrates the way he combines syntactic units: "If the fathers do any where, as oftentimes they doe, make the true visible Church of Christ and hereticall companies opposite, they are to be construed as separating heretikes not altogether from the companie of beleevers, but from the fellowship of sound beleevers" (3.1.11).[3] He begins with a lengthy subordinate clause, lengthened further by inclusion of a parenthetical clause, "as. . . doe," and extends the brief main clause with two balanced and antithetical prepositional phrases. Edelen has shown how Hooker constructs his long Ciceronean sentences through the basic units found in this one, and there is no need to attempt here a further analysis of sentence length. Instead it will be sufficient to give a few examples that illustrate the common rhetorical devices of Hooker's style and to suggest how they contribute to tone.

In a recent analysis Brian Vickers has called attention to the schemes of repetition in Hooker's style—perhaps its single most prominent feature.[4] Among these, the schemes of alliteration, ploce (repetition of a word), polyptoton (repetition of a word in altered grammatical form), balance, antithesis, and chiasmus occur frequently. The following passage serves to illustrate the range of Hooker's use of schemes:

> Dangerous it were for the feeble braine of man to wade
> farre into the doings of the most High, whome although
> to knowe be life, and joy to make mention of his name:
> yet our soundest knowledge is to know that we know him
> not as in deed he is, neither can know him: and our   (5)
>   safest eloquence concerning him is our silence, when
>   we confesse without confession that his glory is
>   inexplicable, his greatnes above our capacitie and
>   reach. He is above, and we upon earth, therefore it
> behoveth our wordes to be warie and fewe. (1.2.2)   (10)

In this passage the word "know" is repeated four times and "confesse without confession" (l. 7) represents polyptoton. The repetition of the infinitive phrases (ll. 3–5) creates balance, whereas the inversion of the order of grammatical elements in line 3 forms chiasmus. The final sentence opens with balanced clauses that also are examples of antithesis (ll. 9–10), and the passage ends with two balanced adjectives, "warie and fewe." Vickers has shown that Hooker uses, in addition to the schemes noted here, anadiplosis (re-

peating the last word of one clause at the beginning of the next),
anaphora (beginning successive clauses with the same word), and
epanalepsis (repeating the first word of a clause at its end).[5] The
schemes of repetition establish a tone which suggests deliberation,
conscious crafting, moderation, reasonable discourse, and control.

Two additional characteristics of Hooker's style illustrated by the
passage are worthy of note. For a writer whose sentences are generally
long, Hooker displays a remarkable amount of omission. In the passage just quoted he omits the verb "be" (1. 3), the pronoun "we"
(1. 5), as well as the verbs "is" (1. 8) and "are" (1. 9). Balanced
constructions with their grammatical units in series invite omission,
which renders the prose more solid. A second notable characteristic,
inversion—usually attributed to the pervasive influence of Latin on
Hooker—enables him to create a wide range of effects. He moves
verbs and adjectives freely for emphasis, the most obvious example
from the quotation occurring in the first line: "Dangerous it were. . . ."
Hooker's prose is filled with sentences which begin with the predicate
adjective—"True it is . . . ," "Capable we are . . . ," and so on. This type
of inversion is found often in the Elizabethan Book of Homilies
(*Certayne Sermons and Homilies*), which may be its source. Through
inversion Hooker succeeds in placing the important word in an em-
phatic position.

A third passage will serve to indicate something about tropes, rhetorical questions, and tone generally:

For doth anie man doubt but that even from the flesh of Christ our verie
bodies doe receive that life which shall make them glorious at the later
daie, and for which they are allreadie accompted partes of his blessed
bodie? Our corruptible bodies could never live the life they shall live,
were it not that heere they are joyned with his bodie which is incorruptible, and that his is in oures as a cause of immortalitie, a cause by remov-
inge through the death and merit of his owne flesh that which hindered
the life of oures. Christ is therefore both as God and as man that true
vine whereof wee both spirituallie and corporallie are branches. (5.56.9)

The passage begins with a rhetorical question, a device that occurs
hundreds of times in *Ecclesiastical Polity*, the brief third book alone
having more than fifty. Rhetorical questions have several functions—
from delivering an ironic rebuke to creating a tone of conciliation.
Hooker uses them for a broad range of purposes, including transition,
but the effect is more often than not one of conciliation. Frequently,

as in the example that begins the passage, he resorts to the device as an indication that he does not want to probe a religious mystery or point of doctrine too deeply. The question suggests that reason has reached its limit and that beyond lies the realm of faith.

Another striking feature of Hooker's style found in the passage is the use of the subjunctive mode, "*were* it not" (italics mine). This grammatical element—like the archaic inflections one encounters so often ("doth") and tmesis ("to God ward")—lends a kind of archaic tone to the style, but it contributes something else as well. Like the rhetorical question it is conciliatory; it contributes to the reasoned, balanced, moderate tone of the work. To see how these devices are reinforced by the schemes of repetition, one can note the light alliteration in the opening question "*f*rom ... *f*lesh" and "*b*lessed *b*odie." The second sentence incorporates skillful polyptoton, "live ... life ... live"; some balance, "death and merit"; and antithesis, "death ... life." The final sentence, in the form of a conclusion, makes use of more complex balancing "both as God and as man," "both spirituallie and corporallie," and striking inversion which intrudes a balanced phrase between the subject and verb of the final clause.

The final sentence introduces the figurative language of the vine and branches, one of Hooker's numerous metaphors. It is possible to read Hooker and miss them, because they are usually conventional or commonplace, frequently derived from the Bible. But, as Vickers demonstrates, Hooker employs a number of vivid metaphors when he is addressing his opponents, many of them colloquial in origin.[6] Similar to the metaphor, personification frequently occurs as a trope but is scarcely noticeable because Hooker expects it to bear conventional meanings only, as this example illustrates: "For that which all men have at all times learned, nature her selfe must needes have taught; and God being the author of nature, her voyce is but his instrument" (1.8.3).

W. Speed Hill points out that for the student of literature, Hooker's style represents the facet of his work with the most insistent claim.[7] But the extent of his stylistic influence on the course of English literature remains uncertain. According to Boswell, Samuel Johnson framed his style upon that of Hooker and others, and Boswell may well have been right. But few writers did, perhaps in part because Hooker made no contribution to the development of a prose genre, unlike the later prose masters—Bacon, Browne, Dryden, Addison, and

Swift. Hooker wrote what, formally, was a treatise, a well-known genre during the Renaissance but one that soon became minor from the standpoint of literary interest.

One does not experience in Hooker's prose the headlong movement of Bacon, the imaginative power of Donne, the baroque splendor of Taylor and Browne, the rich variety of Dryden, the unerring idiomatic sense of Tillotson, not to mention the grace and precision of the Augustans, Swift and Addison. But Hooker does offer prose of dignity and power, richly adorned with rhetorical devices, for its time a prose of unusual clarity. He speaks to his readers through numerous personae, yet remains the teacher, attempting to enlighten and instruct, and to win them over if possible.

Intellectual Legacy

Hooker's intellectual influence and legacy are manifest in such varied branches of learning as history, law, literature, philosophy, political science, and theology. Scholarly journals in these fields include articles on his works, and at major universities one comes to expect library holdings on Hooker to be housed in law and theology libraries as well as in general collections. The breadth of vision which his treatise embodies accounts for its wide appeal. With the possible exception of church history and apologetics, however, Hooker's influence appears to have been broad rather than deep.

In his own time, he did not achieve his main goal of reconciling the Puritans with the national church. As to his secondary purpose, to make obedience to the laws of the Anglican church seem reasonable, it is not readily seen how he might better have succeeded. But in achieving this much, he championed positions that did not appeal to political and religious leaders of the seventeenth century. The ideas of a king under the law, of a national church with a measure of autonomy and customary rights, and of apostolic succession supported only by tradition and practicality would not have been entirely acceptable to Laudian prelates or Stuart monarchs. A new and sterner Puritanism arose, more vigorous than that which Hooker had opposed, with groups united not to impose a presbyterian system but at any cost to rid the country of the hierarchy. In this climate, Anglicans, Puritans, and Catholics could all find support for points of controversy in Hooker, and, as John Booty has shown, they did.[8] By the time he wrote the biography, Walton could cite numerous people who had praised Hooker's work including Charles I and Pope Clement VIII. Catholic apologists found *Ecclesiastical Polity* a rich source of ammunition against Protestants, and James II professed that reading Hooker's work had influenced his conversion to Catholicism. Among the Puritans, Milton, Andrew Marvell, and Richard Baxter cite Hooker favorably. John Locke quotes passages from Hooker in support of his theory of the social contract, attributing to the churchman more agreement than was in reality present.[9] John Dryden acknowledged his debt to Hooker, and his religious poem *Religio Laici* one can detect Hooker's moderate positions.

During the eighteenth century Hooker continued to be read and respected, but he held a less conspicuous place. One kind of exposure that kept Hooker before the reading public is well worth noting. In his *Dictionary* (1755), Samuel Johnson used more than a thousand quotations from Hooker's works, most of them from books 1–4. The numerous citations place him in the company of Bacon, the Bible, Sir Thomas Browne, Dryden, Milton, Pope, and Shakespeare. He represents Johnson's most important source for entries relating to church polity, though by no means is he limited to these. Johnson cites him for numerous common words, especially adverbs, and speaks of him with respect.

The modern scholarly tradition of Hooker studies dates from the edition of John Keble in 1836, which was in its seventh edition by 1888. Keble brought all of the known works together, included related texts by Hooker's contemporaries, and provided extensive editorial apparatus. Hooker has found numerous scholars willing to devote their efforts to understanding and explaining his works. Textual and authorial problems have received careful attention; the uncertainties that remain in these areas may well be resolved by the editors now preparing the Folger Library Edition. A major critical issue has been internal contradictions and inconsistencies perceived in Hooker's political and theological thought by such authors as Alessandro P. d'Entrèves, Peter Munz, Gunnar Hillerdal, and H. F. Kearney. Their objections have been answered by other scholars who find Hooker consistent, among them John Marshall, W. Speed Hill, Egil Grislis, W. D. J. Cargill Thompson, A. S. McGrade, and Olivier Loyer. The question is not entirely settled despite impressive efforts on both sides.[10]

But if one accepts Hooker on his own terms—recognizing that he was obligated to uphold the theology of the Church of England and

the political realities of the English Renaissance—then there appear
to be no serious inconsistencies. If the treatise is regarded as a literary
work, analogous to *The Faerie Queene* or *Paradise Lost*, then a high
degree of unity and coherence becomes evident. As McGrade has
pointed out, Hooker did not pursue philosophical and political questions as deeply as he might have;[11] he was inclined toward, but not
limited by, an approach that pressed questions only as far as necessary
to his polemic purpose. He makes a more responsible use of biblical
and patristic sources than did his Puritan opponents, and he would
have been surprised by any suggestion that he had made discoveries
in theology.

Reading Hooker is an experience which enriches us and repays us
amply. He challenges the reader by the breadth and extent of meanings which he attaches to important terms—"law," "polity," "will,"
"appetite," "church," "reason," "preaching"—a tendency complemented
by his laying down broad principles, like those of book 5, whose
applications are far-reaching. Beneath the surface, ever present, are
assumptions which he seldom articulates but which are central to his
thought—entelechy, hierarchy, freedom of will. On the other hand,
it is well to observe that some words that one associates with Hooker
were not used by him—Anglican, Puritan, and *via media*.

One obtains from Hooker's rationalism a quality not easily found
elsewhere in English literature. It is reminiscent of Sir Thomas
Browne in breadth and spirit of inquiry, without the quaintness and
curiosity that one detects in the prose of Browne. Hooker achieves a
unified intellectual synthesis, remains optimistic about man and his
institutions, and upholds the ideal of an ordered, harmonious, and
hierarchical human existence. The elevation of reason in support of
similar values occurs again during the Enlightenment, but then it
becomes a vehicle for satire, wherein the breadth of vision, the
solidity, or both, are diminished. To find a work of similar intellectual
breadth one must examine Pope's *Essay on Man*; viewed in the light
of this comparison, the soundness of Hooker's achievement becomes
evident.

Where institutions and laws are concerned, Hooker shows himself
conservative, in keeping with his times and his background. He would
have agreed with Bagehot that an imperfect law is preferable to no
law. Although his profound grasp of ecclesiastical history impressed
upon him that institutions, like men, must develop and change, he
believed that progress best occurred in an atmosphere of moderation

and reason. He reflects a moderate, rational ideal in his work by seeking the middle way between extremes, by arguing from broad principles clearly stated, by justifying what exists through examining its causes, by offering compromises and concessions when he believes them beneficial, and by recoiling from abstruse theological points which he regards as nonessential or indifferent. With Burke, he would have thought the inclination to preserve and the ability to improve the two most important traits of a statesman.

Notes and References

Chapter One

1. Izaak Walton, *The Life of Mr. Richard Hooker*, in *The Works of That Learned and Judicious Divine Mr. Richard Hooker, with an Account of His Life and Death by Isaac Walton*, ed. John Keble, rev. R. W. Church and F. Paget, 7th ed., 3 vols. (London, 1888; reprint, New York: Burt Franklin, 1970), 1:6. Quotations from Walton's biography and of other biographical matter will be from Keble's edition and will be cited in the text by volume and page numbers.

2. Among John Hooker's impressive antiquarian endeavors, records of Exeter hold a significant place, especially his description of the municipal duties of officials in *The Offices of Excester* (1584) and his *Catalog of the Bishops of Excester* (1584). The *Offices* has been edited and published in *Elizabethan Backgrounds*, ed. Arthur F. Kinney (Hamden, Conn.: Shoe String Press, 1975), pp. 106–37. The most significant source of biographical information about John Hooker is his *The Life and Times of Sir Peter Carew*, ed. John Maclean (London, 1857).

3. J. H. Bernard, "The Father of Richard Hooker," *Irish Church Quarterly* 6 (1913):267–68.

4. Thomas Fowler, *The History of Corpus Christi College with Lists of Its Members* (Oxford: Clarendon Press, 1893), p. 148.

5. Ibid., pp. 149–51.

6. Ibid., p. 128.

7. Ronald Bayne, "Hooker," in *Encyclopaedia of Religion and Ethics*, ed. James Hastings (New York: Charles Scribner's Sons, 1914), 6:773.

8. C. J. Sisson, *The Judicious Marriage of Mr. Hooker and the Birth of "The Laws of Ecclesiastical Polity"* (Cambridge: Cambridge University Press, 1940), pp. 17–44.

9. S. J. Knox, *Walter Travers: Paragon of Elizabethan Puritanism* (London: Methuen & Co., 1962), p. 56.

10. Ibid., p. 59.

11. Thomas Fuller, *History of the Worthies of England*, ed. P. A. Nuttall, 3 vols. (New York: AMS Press, 1965), 1:423.

12. Thomas Fuller, *The Church-History of Britain from the Birth of Jesus Christ Untill the Year MDCXLVII* (London: J. Williams, 1655), 3:216.

13. Ibid.

14. Knox, p. 77.

15. Ibid., p. 78.
16. Ibid., p. 145.
17. Sisson, p. 21.
18. Ibid., p. 24.
19. Ibid., p. 25.
20. Rudolph Almasy, "Richard Hooker's Address to the Presbyterians," *Anglican Theological Review* 61 (1979):463.
21. Sisson, p. 59.
22. Rosemary Keen, "Inventory of Richard Hooker, 1601," *Archeologia Cantiana* 70 (1956):231.

Chapter Two

1. Some fragments in manuscript have been discovered in recent years. A fragmentary outline of *Ecclesiastical Polity*, Book VIII, has been published by P. G. Stanwood, "The Richard Hooker Manuscripts," *Long Room* 11 (1975):7–10, and fragments of sermons and notes are described by P. G. Stanwood and Laetitia Yeandle, "Three Manuscript Sermon Fragments by Richard Hooker," *Manuscripta* 21, (1977):33–37 and "An Autograph Manuscript by Richard Hooker," *Manuscripta* 18 (1974):38–42.
2. *Works*, ed. John Keble, 3:470. Citations from the minor works will be from Keble's edition and will be cited in the text by volume and page numbers.
3. Professor Hill designates this as a compilation of three sermons in series and points out that it was printed in a second edition within a year following the first edition of 1612. See W. Speed Hill, "The Evolution of Hooker's *Laws of Ecclesiastical Polity*," in *Studies in Richard Hooker*, ed. W. Speed Hill, (Cleveland: Case Western Reserve University Press, 1972), p. 124.
4. Michael T. Malone classifies Hooker's view of predestination as "semi-Arminian, semi-Calvinist" and points out that his distinction between God's primary or general will that all be saved and a secondary or occasional will that the elect be saved involves a circular argument. See "The Doctrine of Predestination in the Thought of William Perkins and Richard Hooker," *Anglican Theological Review* 52 (1970):117.

Chapter Three

1. Sisson, pp. 64–65.
2. W. Speed Hill, ed. *The Folger Library Edition of the Works of Richard Hooker*, 6 vols. (Cambridge: Harvard University Press, Belknap Press, 1977–), vol. 1, ed. Georges Edelen (1977), Preface, 1.1. Quota-

tions from Hooker's works in this chapter will be from Hill's edition and will be cited in the text by book, chapter, and paragraph numbers.

3. *Works*, ed. Keble, 1:177.

4. C. S. Lewis, *English Literature in the Sixteenth Century Excluding Drama*, O.H.E.L., vol. 3 (Oxford: Clarendon Press, 1954), p. 453.

5. "The Historical Perspective of Richard Hooker: A Renaissance Paradox," *Journal of Medieval and Renaissance Studies* 3 (1973):47–48.

6. E. N. S. Thompson, "Richard Hooker among the Controversialists," *Philological Quarterly* 20 (1941):460.

Chapter Four

1. Bodleian Ad. MS C. 165.

2. *Works*, ed. Hill, 2:2. Quotations in this chapter will be from Hill's edition and will be cited in the text by book, chapter, and paragraph numbers.

Chapter Five

1. On the question of composition of the books see W. Speed Hill, "The Evolution of Hooker's *Laws of Ecclesiastical Polity*" in *Studies in Richard Hooker*, ed. Hill, pp. 132–34.

2. Sisson, pp. 85–86, 98.

3. Ibid., p. 108.

4. Cranmer's letter is traditionally dated 1598, though Hardin Craig argues in support of an earlier dating. See "*Of the Laws of Ecclesiastical Polity*—First Form," *Journal of the History of Ideas* 5 (1944):100–101.

5. *Works*, ed. Keble, 2:608. Quotations in this chapter will be from Keble's edition and will be cited in the text by volume and page numbers.

6. R. A. Houk, ed., *Hooker's Ecclesiastical Polity, Book VIII* (New York: Columbia University Press, 1931), pp. 70–71.

7. Ibid., p. 72.

8. *Works*, ed. Keble, 1:xli.

9. Houk, pp. 82–90. For a recent article giving reasons in support of Houk's view see Arthur S. McGrade, "Repentance and Spiritual Power: Book VI of Richard Hooker's *Of the Laws of Ecclesiastical Polity*," *Journal of Ecclesiastical History* 29 (1978):163–76.

10. Ibid., pp. 89–90.

Chapter Six

1. See especially Sister M. Stephanie Stueber, "The Balanced Diction of Hooker's *Polity*," *PMLA* 71 (1956):808–26; W. Speed Hill, "The

Authority of Hooker's Style," *Studies in Philology* 67 (1970):328–38; Georges Edelen, "Hooker's Style," in *Studies in Richard Hooker*, ed. Hill, pp. 241–77; and Brian Vickers, "Hooker's Prose Style," in *Of the Laws of Ecclesiastical Polity: An Abridged Edition*, by Richard Hooker, ed. A. S. McGrade and Brian Vickers (New York: St. Martin's Press, 1975), pp. 41–59.

2. Edelen, p. 241.

3. Quotations from Hooker's *Works* in this chapter are from Hill's edition and will be cited in the text by book, chapter, and paragraph numbers.

4. Vickers, pp. 49, 52.

5. Ibid., pp. 51–52.

6. Ibid., p. 54.

7. Hill, p. 328.

8. See John E. Booty, "Hooker and Anglicanism," in *Studies in Richard Hooker*, ed. Hill, pp. 241–77.

9. George Bull, "What Did Locke Borrow from Hooker?" *Thought* 7 (1932):134–35.

10. See A. P. d'Entrèves, *The Medieval Contribution to Political Thought* (Oxford: Oxford University Press, 1939); Peter Munz, *The Place of Hooker in the History of Thought* (London: Routledge & Kegan Paul, 1952); H. F. Kearney, "Richard Hooker: A Reconstruction," *Cambridge Journal*, 5 (1952):300–11. The more significant defenses of the unity of Hooker's thought are the following: John Marshall, *Hooker and the Anglican Tradition* (Sewanee, Tenn.: University of the South Press and London: Adam & Charles Block, 1963); A. S. McGrade, "The Coherence of Hooker's Polity: The Books on Power," *Journal of the History of Ideas*, 24 (1963):163–82; Egil Grislis, "Richard Hooker's Image of Man," in *Renaissance Papers*, 1963, ed. S. K. Heninger, *et al.* (The Southeastern Renaissance Conference, 1964), pp. 73–84; W. Speed Hill, "Doctrine and Polity in Hooker's *Laws*," *English Literary Renaissance*, 2 (1972):173–93; W. D. J. Cargill Thompson, "The Philosopher of the 'Politic Society,'" in *Studies in Richard Hooker*, ed. Hill, pp. 3–76; and Olivier Loyer, *L'Anglicanisme de Richard Hooker* 2 vols. (Paris: Libraire Honoré Champion, 1979).

11. Arthur S. McGrade, "Introduction 1," in Richard Hooker, *Of the Laws of Ecclesiastical Polity: An Abridged Edition*, ed. A. S. McGrade and Brian Vickers (New York: St. Martin's Press, 1975), pp. 37–38.

Selected Bibliography

PRIMARY SOURCES

1. Principal Sixteenth- and Seventeenth-Century Editions

Of the Lawes of Ecclesiasticall Politie, Eyght Bookes. London: John Windet, [1593]. Includes the preface and books 1–4.

Of the Lawes of Ecclesiasticall Politie: The Fift Booke. London: John Windet, 1597.

Of the Lawes of Ecclesiasticall Politie: The Sixth and Eighth Books. London: Richard Bishop, 1648.

Of the Lawes of Ecclesiastical Politie. London: Andrew Crooke, 1661[2]. Includes Gauden's biography and the first publication of book 7, as well as the tractates.

Of the Lawes of Ecclesiastical Politie. London: Andrew Crooke, 1666. Includes Walton's biography.

2. Principal Modern Editions

The Works of That Learned and Judicious Divine Mr. Richard Hooker: With an Account of His Life and Death by Isaac Walton. Edited by John Keble, revised by R. W. Church and F. Paget. 7th ed. 3 vols. Oxford: Clarendon Press, 1888. Reprint. New York: Burt Franklin, 1970. The most nearly complete and the standard scholarly edition.

Of the Laws of Ecclesiastical Polity: The Fifth Book. Edited by Ronald Bayne. English Theological Library. London: Macmillan, 1902. Contains an excellent essay on Elizabethan Puritanism and extensive editorial apparatus. Reprints *A Christian Letter* (1599), the attack on Hooker.

Hooker's Ecclesiastical Polity: Book VIII. Edited by Raymond Aaron Houk. New York: Columbia University Press, 1931. Upholds the authenticity of the final books and offers hypotheses about their composition.

Of the Lawes of Ecclesiasticall Politie: Books I–V, [1594]–1597. Menston, England: Scolar Press, 1969. A facsimile reprint.

Of the Laws of Ecclesiastical Polity: An Abridged Edition. Edited by A. S. McGrade and Brian Vickers. New York: St. Martin's Press, 1975. One of many abridgments, this edition includes valuable introductions by the editors.

The Folger Library Edition of the Works of Richard Hooker. Edited by
W. Speed Hill. 6 vols. Cambridge: Harvard University Press, Belknap Press, 1977–. Published: vol. 1, ed. Georges Edelen (1977),
and vol. 2, ed. W. Speed Hill (1977); vol. 3, ed. P. G. Stanwood
(1981). When complete, this edition will replace Keble.

SECONDARY SOURCES

1. Books
Covel, William. *A Just and Temperate Defence of the Five Books Of Ec-
clesistical Policie . . . : Against an Uncharitable Letter of Certain English Protestants. . . .* London, 1603. A point-by-point analysis of an
attack on Hooker, *A Christian Letter.* The Puritan attack is reprinted
in the Bayne edition of book 5, cited above.
Davies, E. T. *The Political Ideas of Richard Hooker.* London: S.P.C.K.,
1948. A brief, generalized, and readable account.
D'Entrèves, A. P. *The Medieval Contribution to Political Thought: Thomas
Aquinas, Marsilius of Padua, Richard Hooker.* Oxford: Oxford University Press, 1939. An important study of Hooker's political ideas,
with reference to Renaissance thought.
————. *Riccardo Hooker: Contributo alla teoria e alla storia del diritto
naturale.* R. Università di Torino, Memorie dell'Istituto Giuridico,
ser. 2, no. 22. Turin: Presso L'Istituto Giuridico della R. Università,
1932. Places Hooker in the natural-law tradition and emphasizes his
debt to medieval thought.
Dirksen, Cletus F. *A Critical Analysis of Richard Hooker's Theory of the
Relation of Church and State.* Notre Dame: University of Notre
Dame Press, 1947. Examines the historical and theological background of England in Hooker's time and concludes that he provided a theoretical foundation for an expedient Establishment.
Fowler, Thomas. *The History of Corpus Christi College with Lists of Its
Members.* Oxford: Clarendon Press, 1893. Biographical information
on Hooker at Corpus Christi.
Fuller, Thomas. *The Church-History of Britain from the Birth of Jesus
Christ Untill the Year MDCXLVII.* London: J. Williams, 1655. Brief
but memorable biographical and critical comments.
Grislis, Egil, and Hill, W. Speed. *Richard Hooker: A Selected Bibliography.* Pittsburgh: Clifford E. Barbour Library, 1971. The most extensive bibliography available, its three sections are devoted to editions,
secondary works principally on Hooker, and works dealing briefly
with Hooker.
Hill, W. Speed. *Richard Hooker: A Descriptive Bibliography of the Early*

Editions: 1593–1724. Cleveland: Case Western Reserve University Press, 1970. Essential bibliography for the serious scholar.

———. *Studies in Richard Hooker: Essays Preliminary to an Edition of His Works.* Cleveland: Case Western Reserve University Press, 1972. The most important critical book on Hooker which includes six essays on major topics and an excellent annotated bibliography.

Hillerdal, Gunnar. *Reason and Revelation in Richard Hooker.* Lunds Universitets Arsskrift, n.s. 1, vol. 54, no. 7. Lund: C. W. K. Gleerup, 1962. A study of Hooker's theology by a Lutheran scholar.

Hooker, John. *The Life and Times of Sir Peter Carew.* Edited by John Maclean. London: Bell & Daldy, 1857. Biographical information on Hooker's uncle and father.

Knox, S. J. *Walter Travers: Paragon of Elizabeth Puritanism.* London: Methuen & Co., 1962. Biographical account of Hooker at the Temple.

Loyer, Olivier. *L'Anglicanisme de Richard Hooker.* 2 vols. Paris: Librarie Honoré Champion, 1979. Topical and thematic analysis of Hooker's work, defends his consistency.

Marshall, John S. *Hooker and the Anglican Tradition: An Historical and Theological Study of Hooker's Ecclesiastical Polity.* Sewanee, Tenn.: University Press at the University of the South, 1963. Important account of Hooker's thought, his work seen as an Anglican *summa*.

Munz, Peter. *The Place of Hooker in the History of Thought.* London: Routledge & Kegan Paul, 1952. A thorough account of Hooker's debts to classical, patristic, and Renaissance sources.

Novarr, David. *The Making of Walton's Lives.* Cornell Studies in English, no. 41. Ithaca: Cornell University Press, 1958. Scholarly investigation of Walton's art of biography.

Pollard, Arthur. *Richard Hooker.* Writers and Their Work, no. 195. London: Longmans, Green, & Co., 1966. Useful introduction.

Shirley, F. J. *Richard Hooker and Contemporary Political Ideas.* London: S.P.C.K., 1949. Compares Hooker's political ideas to those of Protestants and Catholics of his time, and finds that he contributed to the development of liberalism.

Sisson, C. J. *The Judicious Marriage of Mr. Hooker and the Birth of "The Laws of Ecclesiastical Polity."* Cambridge: Cambridge University Press, 1940. Valuable biographical information on Hooker's marriage, family, and friends. Thorough investigation of the composition and publication of his treatise.

Thornton, Lionel S. *Richard Hooker: A Study of His Theology.* English Theologians. London: S.P.C.K., 1924. Examines major theological topics in Hooker.

2. Articles

Almasy, Rudolph. "The Purpose of Richard Hooker's Polemic." *Journal of the History of Ideas* 39 (1978):251–70. Believes Hooker directs his polemic against Cartwright and continues the Whitgift-Cartwright controversy.

————. "Richard Hooker's Address to the Presbyterians." *Anglican Theological Review* 61 (1979):462–74. Contrasts Hooker's polemic approach with that of his contemporaries and describes his attitudes toward opponents.

Avis, P. D. L. "Richard Hooker and John Calvin." *Journal of Ecclesiastical History* 32 (1981):19–28. Surveys Hooker's remarks on Calvin and finds them balanced. The article is followed by "Richard Hooker and John Calvin: A Comment" by Richard Bauckham (pp. 29–33) relating Hooker's attitudes toward Calvin to his view of reformers generally.

Bauckham, Richard. "Hooker, Travers, and the Church of Rome in the 1580's." *Journal of Ecclesiastical History* 29 (1978):37–50. Examines anti-Catholic statements in the Sermons and concludes that Hooker's tolerance of Catholicism is minimal.

Bayne, Ronald. "Hooker." In *Encyclopaedia of Religion and Ethics*, edited by James Hastings. New York: Charles Scribner's Sons, 1914, 6:772–76. Perhaps the most valuable brief biographical account.

Bernard, J. H. "The Father of Richard Hooker." *Irish Church Quarterly* 6 (1913):265–70. Biographical information on the career of Roger Hooker in Ireland.

Booty, John. "The Quest for the Historical Hooker." *The Churchman* 80 (1966):185–93. Biographical details and perspective on major controversies related to Hooker's *Works*.

————. "Richard Hooker." In *The Spirit of Anglicanism*, edited by William J. Wolf. Wilton, Conn.: Morehouse-Barlow Co., 1979, pp. 1–48. Finds continuing religious significance in Hooker's *Works*.

Bull, George. "What Did Locke Borrow from Hooker?" *Thought* 7 (1932):122–35. Locke's borrowings distort Hooker's meanings and intentions about government.

Cohen, Eileen Z. "The Visible Solemnity: Ceremony and Order in Shakespeare and Hooker." *Texas Studies in Literature and Language* 12 (1970):181–95. Themes similar to Hooker's are found in Shakespeare's second tetralogy.

Craig, Hardin. "*Of the Laws of Ecclesiastical Polity*—First Form." *Journal of the History of Ideas* 5 (1944):91–104. Argues that Hooker's treatise was essentially complete in 1593 but that he expanded book 5 during revision.

Croxford, Leslie. "The Originality of Hooker's Work." *Proceedings of the*

Leeds Philosophical and Literary Society 15, pt. 2 (1973):15–57. Shows that Hooker expanded the meanings of key Thomistic terms like "reason," "law," and "church" but rejected the correspondence theory of church-state derived from St. Thomas.

De Lara, Dionisio. "Richard Hooker's Concept of Law." *Anglican Theological Review* 44 (1962):380–89. Discusses the meaning of "law" in *Ecclesiastical Polity*, book 1.

Ferguson, Arthur B. "The Historical Perspective of Richard Hooker: A Renaissance Paradox." *Journal of Medieval and Renaissance Studies* 3 (1973):17–49. Analyzes Hooker's views of social and political change, shows how he differs with Aquinas.

Grislis, Egil. "Richard Hooker's Image of Man." In *Renaissance Papers, 1963,* edited by S. K. Heninger, Jr., et al. Southeastern Renaissance Conference, 1964, pp. 73–84. Response to Hillerdal on reason and grace.

———. "Richard Hooker's Method of Theological Inquiry." *Anglican Theological Review* 45 (1963):190–203. Scripture, reason, and consensus are examined as bases for inquiry.

———. "The Role of Consensus in Richard Hooker's Method of Theological Inquiry." In *The Heritage of Christian Thought: Essays in Honor of Robert Lowry Calhoun,* edited by Robert E. Cushman and Egil Grislis. New York: Harper & Row, 1965, pp. 64–88. Explores Hooker's efforts to apply a classical view of consensus to the formulation of doctrine and finds him responsive to change.

Hill, W. Speed. "The Authority of Hooker's Style." *Studies in Philology* 67 (1970):328–38. Finds important unique stylistic elements in Hooker's *Sermons.*

———. "Doctrine and Polity in Hooker's *Laws.*" *English Literary Renaissance* 2 (1972):173–93. Finds the positions in Hooker's minor works consistent with those of the *Laws.*

———. "Hooker's Polity: The Problem of the 'Three Last Books.'" *Huntington Library Quarterly* 34 (1971):317–36. Upholds the authenticity of the final three books and agrees with Keble that Hooker did not intend book 6 as it stands as a part of his treatise.

———. "Hooker's 'Preface' Chapters VIII and IX." *Notes and Queries,* n.s. 16 (1969):457–59. Concerns a later publication of the two final chapters of Hooker's preface.

Kearney, H. F. "Richard Hooker: A Reconstruction." *Cambridge Journal* 5 (1952):300–311. Finds conflict in Hooker between the influence of Aquinas and that of Marsilio of Padua on law.

Keen, Rosemary. "Inventory of Richard Hooker, 1601." *Archeologia Cantiana* 70 (1956):231–36. Itemized list of Hooker's possessions at death and their value.

Looten, C. "Un avocat de l'Église anglicane: Richard Hooker (1554–1600): Of the Laws of Ecclesiastical Polity (1592–3 et 1597)." Revue d'Histoire Ecclesiastique 33 (1937):485–534. Generalized account of the life and works.

Mahon, Vincent. "The 'Christian Letter': Some Puritan Objections to Hooker's Work; and Hooker's 'Undressed' Comments." Review of English Studies 25 (1974):305–12. A discussion of style and proposal for a modern edition of A Christian Letter.

McGrade, Arthur S. "The Coherence of Hooker's Polity: The Books on Power." Journal of the History of Ideas 24 (1963):163–82. Largely concerns distinctions of law and authority in book 8, finds the books consistent and coherent.

———. "The Public and the Religious in Hooker's Polity." Church History 37 (1968):404–22. Discusses organization and purposes of book 5.

———. "Repentance and Spiritual Power: Book VI of Richard Hooker's Of the Laws of Ecclesiastical Polity." Journal of Ecclesiastical History 29 (1978):163–76. Makes the case for book 6 as an intended part of Hooker's treatise.

Malone, Michael T. "The Doctrine of Predestination in the Thought of William Perkins and Richard Hooker." Anglican Theological Review 52 (1970):103–17. Analyzes passages in Hooker dealing with the theological doctrine.

Marshall, John S. "Hooker's Doctrine of God." Anglican Theological Review 29 (1947):81–88. The concept of God as related to law, personal attributes, and divine character.

———. "Hooker's Theory of Church and State." Anglican Theological Review 27 (1945):151–60. Hooker's view becomes the Anglican view of church-state relations.

Smith, Elsie. "Hooker at Salisbury." Times Literary Supplement, 30 March 1962, p. 223. Cites evidence supporting the view that Hooker resided at Boscombe.

Stanwood, P. G. "The Richard Hooker Manuscripts." Long Room 11 (1975):7–10. A recently discovered manuscript outline of Hooker's eighth book is described.

———, and Yeandle, Laetitia. "An Autograph Manuscript by Richard Hooker." Manuscripta 18 (1974):38–42. Analysis of a manuscript draft of "Of the Nature of Pride"; supports the authenticity of two letters to Rainolds.

———, and Yeandle, Laetitia. "Richard Hooker's Use of Thomas More." Moreana 35 (1972):5–16. Explains Hooker's attitudes toward More.

———, and Yeandle, Laetitia. "Three Manuscript Sermon Fragments by Richard Hooker." Manuscripta 21 (1977):33–37. Manuscripts of three sermon fragments in James Ussher's hand are attributed to Hooker.

Stueber, Sister M. Stephanie. "The Balanced Diction of Hooker's *Polity*." *PMLA* 71 (1956):808–26. Hooker's style found appropriate to his Christian humanism.

Surlis, Paul. "Natural Law in Richard Hooker (c. 1554–1600)." *Irish Church Quarterly* 35 (1968):173–85. Surveys Hooker's view of natural law topically.

Tebeaux, Elizabeth. "Donne and Hooker on the Nature of Man: The Diverging 'Middle Way.'" *Restoration Quarterly* 24 (1981):29–44. Explains differences in their reliance on reason.

Thompson, E. N. S. "Richard Hooker among the Controversialists." *Philological Quarterly* 20 (1941):454–64. Hooker rose above the controversy of his day.

Woodhouse, H. F. "Permanent Features of Hooker's Polity." *Anglican Theological Review* 42 (1960):164–68. Finds value in Hooker's sense of proportion, establishment of broad principles, search for truth, and respect for antiquity.

Index